THE 200% LIFE

THE 200% LIFE

YOUR GUIDE TO SPIRITUAL GROWTH & BUSINESS SUCCESS
WITHOUT MEDITATING ON A MOUNTAINTOP

ADAM HERGENROTHER

WITH HALLIE WARNER

ADAM HERGENROTHER COMPANIES

THE 200% LIFE

Your Guide To Spiritual Growth and Business Success Without Meditating On A Mountaintop

Cover design by Deaven Palm Lowery
Interior layout design by Dave Marayag

FIRST EDITION

ISBN   979-8-9888313-0-3 *Paperback*

979-8-9888313-1-0 *Hardcover*

979-8-9888313-3-4 *Ebook*

979-8-9888313-2-7 *Audible*

To the next generation of leaders and spiritual seekers.

Contents

Part Four: Absolute Freedom

Author's Note

The 200% Life is the culmination of the decades I've spent studying many spiritual masters, my lived experience, and my spiritual insights and growth. You will find some repetition throughout the chapters, which serves to emphasize some challenging spiritual concepts and ideas that are contradictory to how most of us have been taught to live. I don't consider myself an enlightened individual or a person who has "made it." Simply put I am an ordinary individual seeking the truth of who am I. I still get stuck, I mess up, I overreact, I raise my voice at times, and it's then I realize how long and hard this path is!

This book also reflects the intense work I have done by applying Michael Singer's spiritual teachings over the past fifteen years. There is no way I would be where I am today without the immense impact he has had on my life, along with the influence of many other spiritual thought leaders past and present. My goal with this book is to bring more awareness to these teachings while providing a fresh look at leadership in the business community and to help all people live more peaceful and fuller lives by making ancient spiritual teachings easy to digest and to apply in this modern world.

Another person who has made a substantial contribution to this book is my long-time Chief of Staff, Hallie Warner. Hallie worked by my side for thirteen years helping me to explore these spiritual teachings and apply them to the business world. What you are about to read in the upcoming pages has been edited by Hallie and enhanced by her talent for asking insightful questions, fostering a deeper conversation, and maintaining an unwavering commitment to clarity.

My hope is that this book opens your mind and heart to a different way of living, where you find love, joy, and enthusiasm from within, and carry it with you at all times. If you finish this book and understand it is possible to have inner peace and external success, and you wholeheartedly commit yourself to the work, your journey is bound to surpass your most massive goals. Enjoy the ride! Namaste.

Introduction

The summit is for the ego. The journey is for the soul.
—Author Unknown

It's 4:45 a.m. Your alarm goes off and you're out of bed in sixty seconds or less. It's your first victory of the day. You haven't hit snooze in over a year and you're not going to break that streak now. You have now firmly cemented your spot in the "Up Before 5 a.m. Club." It's snowing outside and a few inches of powder have accumulated on your deck overnight. No matter. You head outside barefoot, channeling Wim Hof, while you breathe deeply for the next four minutes. Back inside, you grab a cup of black coffee and head to your home office. Your phone is sitting on its charger, but you walk by and settle into your leather chair in the corner. Glancing at your watch (it's 5 a.m.), you close your eyes and slowly start to focus on your mantra as you practice Transcendental Meditation for the next twenty minutes. You don't need an alarm. You've been practicing Transcendental Meditation twice a day for almost ten years; your body knows what to do.

Twenty minutes is up and it's time to skim your phone for any text messages. There is one from your mom asking about plans for the holiday and another from your skiing buddy looking to meet up that weekend. No emergencies. Your team has you covered for the most part, anyway. Ah, the sweet power of leverage!

You move over to your desk and open up your laptop, sipping your perfectly cooled coffee. For the next thirty minutes, you journal your thoughts, feelings, ideas, and challenges. It's here every morning that you get clear and centered.

Next, you check a few emails and send off some ideas and check in with your team to make sure they are clear on any new priorities for the day.

By 6 a.m., it's time to exercise. You lace up your Brooks Adrenaline GTS running shoes and start off with a brisk jog on the treadmill while listening to the latest podcast episode of "Masters of Scale" with Reid Hoffman. You follow that with an indoor bike ride on your Wahoo Fitness Kickr Smart Trainer with Zwift on your iPad and then fifteen minutes on the Tonal. Workout complete, you head to the kitchen to have breakfast—always some sort of green smoothie—with your family. By 8 a.m., the kids have headed off to school, your wife is in her office working with her coaching clients, and you're on the way to the office.

For the next three or so hours, it's go time. You record a podcast interview for one of the top ten entrepreneurship podcasts on Spotify, you meet with your Chief of Staff to discuss next year's strategic planning, you get the official "yes" from five new business partners who will be joining your network, you sign the final M&A document to add a new line of business to your organization, and you hear back from a Fortune 500 company that they would like to book you as their keynote speaker for Q2. It's not even noon yet and you've accomplished more than most people do in a month!

You take a brief pause around noon to meditate again for twenty minutes and eat your usual lunch of Ezekial bread, avocado, tomato, spinach, and chickpeas, with a side of black cherry Waterloo sparkling water. You clear out your inbox and then the rest of the day continues much the same as the morning. You approve some final designs for the office renovation, you teach an hour seminar to the new leaders in your company, you meet 1:1 with your CFO and CEO, and you record one more podcast episode to promote your upcoming book launch.

Tonight you leave the office a little bit early because all three of your kids received exemplary report cards, and you're taking them all out to the local rock climbing gym to celebrate while your wife puts together a health protocol for her final client of the day.

As the kids are winding down for the evening, you receive an email that your offer was accepted and you can't wait to tell your wife the news. Annual family vacations in Costa Rica at your very own beach front villa await!

9 p.m. rolls around and it's time to go to bed. You make sure your EightSleep is properly set to 50 degrees, your fan is on, your alarm is set (just in case), your phone is in the other room, your weighted blanket is ready to go, and your sleep tracker is set to on. Optimal sleep for an optimal life. You hit the button on the remote and your electronic shades slowly whirl down and block out the light from the full moon. It's lights out.

And then your mind switches on.

You feel restless, unhappy, and unfulfilled. You just had what most people would call an exceptionally successful and productive day. Your business is growing. Your team is helping you navigate all the challenges that come your way. Your family is thriving. You have optimized your morning and evening routines almost to the minute. You just bought a beach house, for god's sake! You have everything you could possibly want.

But your mind won't stop telling you that it's not enough, that you could do more, have more, and be more to more people. If only you had signed that sixth new business partner today and hadn't lost out on that other offer you made on the ski lodge in Jackson Hole. And you know you could have run two more miles this morning. No worries. You'll get after it tomorrow. You'll be fine once you get a few more business partners signed, and if the Jackson Hole house doesn't work out, that's okay, you'll get the truck you wanted and a boat for the villa.

IS THIS ALL THERE IS?

This is the daily struggle and cycle that most of us experience throughout our lives. You may have accomplished "it all." Or, you may still be in the early stages of your career or business. Either way, the mental and emotional suffering remains the same. We are perpetually dissatisfied and think that the only way to fix that is by chasing the next shiny object (a car, a house, a promotion, a new relationship, etc.).

But at some point, you're going to hit a wall where the search for "more" just doesn't do it for you any longer. And you start to look around and realize there may be another path to get what you're after. You will never be able to find true happiness and fulfillment by chasing external successes and material items. After all, the external world is only 100% of the puzzle.

There is a whole other 100% of life that we ignore or deem too insignificant to put any real effort into. But it actually has everything to do with our fulfillment and happiness! Your inner world is the other 100% of the puzzle. And it's working on the internal world that will ultimately unlock everything you've been looking for all along.

We live in a 200% world.

We have all lived almost exclusively in the 100% external world for far too long. We will not forget the external world. It will still be there for us to enjoy and play with. But it's time to expand our awareness, open our hearts, and dive into a whole other world that is available to us where we will find true happiness and absolute freedom.

Let us begin.

Part One
The 200% Life

What is The 200% Life?

Your outer journey may contain a million steps; your inner journey only has one: the step you are taking right now.

—Eckhart Tolle

Every day within about an hour of waking up, I journal as part of my morning routine. And I ask myself the same question every time: "How do I want to feel today?" The question is designed to remind me of what is important in my life. It is a signpost to aim higher. It's a daily reminder that while the outside world is amazing, what really matters is the inner experience.

Yes, the physical world is beautiful! But it is just secondary to my inner life. Focusing on the external is just an indirect (and much longer!) way of getting what you want.

But if I start my days knowing I want to feel joy, enthusiasm, and inspiration, then I can go play in the big, wild world and experience all the things life has to offer—business challenges, carpooling with the kids, hiking with my wife, training a new puppy, firing an employee, teaching a class, losing money, building a house…whatever! I know that I could walk away from it all and still feel the same inside.

Look, I'm not perfect at this. I don't feel joy and enthusiasm in every moment of every day. But if I can orient my life in that direction, why wouldn't I? Why wouldn't you? It's called a spiritual *practice* and spiritual *journey* for a reason. By positioning myself this way each morning, it gives me so much freedom to just go enjoy life, however it unfolds, instead of making my life about what I can control and what I can get out of it. Life owes us nothing. Period.

When you are just dipping your toes in the water of spiritual growth, the idea of living in two worlds sounds a little out there. We are so connected to our mind and the material world that it's hard to really understand that there is a whole 100% inner world available to us.

This might make it a bit easier to understand. At a recent Project|U event (a year-long full-immersion business and spirituality coaching program that I host), our participants were experiencing a past-life regression session. In the external world, we were all in the same room. We could hear soft music playing in the background. We could feel the chairs we were sitting in. We smelled lunch being prepared in the room next door. We watched the fluorescent lights dim. We listened to the past-life regression guide speak. We were all having an almost identical physical experience. That's the 100% external world.

But inside, in the 100% inner world, the experiences couldn't be more different. Participants traveled back to ancient cultures. One person was a nun raising children in an orphanage, another was a warrior in Britannia. One was a child watching her father die, and someone else was royalty in Egypt. It doesn't even really matter if that past life was true. The experience was real. There were various unique thoughts, feelings, and energy releases happening inside, all while we sat in the same room. That's the 100% internal world.

If that doesn't illustrate that we live in a 200% world, I don't know what does!

THE INWARD JOURNEY

The inner world offers us a whole new space to explore. A space you may have been ignoring for far too long on your quest for success (external success, that is). So, what does it mean to start looking inward?

It just means that you realize the external world is not who you are. That material things are not who you are. That building companies is not who you are. That being a father is not who you are. That being a husband or leader is not who you are. Those are just roles that you take in the external world. We need those roles to help us navigate the human experience, but don't think for a second that what you *do* is who you really are.

At this point in my spiritual journey, it is so clear to me that I am not any of the identities above. It's as clear to me as it is to you that you are not your car, or you are not your shoes. Of course you're not! I also know that I am not my heart or my body or my mind. I am none of those things and all of those things. From this place, when you take your attention from the outside world and turn your gaze inward, the journey begins.

What you are searching for is not outside, it's inside, and it's been there all along.

While my spiritual journey started almost twenty years ago, I'm still learning and growing and letting go every day. Let me take you back a few years.

SPIRITUALITY IS SEQUENTIAL

In January 2013, I sent an email to one of my mentors who has made an indelible impact on my business and spiritual growth. I wrote:

> Over the past couple of years I have made significant changes in my life. I realized a couple of years ago

that I was striving for success for the wrong reasons. Significance was an emotion I set out to achieve through material items. The reality was that I was really insecure with who I was and I was afraid to be myself, so I created a separate identity that was entirely ego-based, and I did everything possible to continue to maintain that identity—including material/economic success.

With this new awareness I set out to figure out why I was acting this way. I immersed myself in books/seminars and conversations that related to this question and started teaching it (hence MindSpark, which I founded last year). However, I really feel I started MindSpark with the wrong intentions—again, more ego/significance-based. The interesting thing is, the minute I made the decision (diffusing the ego, if you will) to shut MindSpark down, the minute things started to become clearer and my purpose of teaching took on a different meaning. One that I've never experienced before. A feeling of giving from a place of non-judgment. This has continued and I've immersed myself even more on my spiritual quest and really bringing this in a teachable format—more in a month than I did the entire time I had MindSpark.

Here are a couple of thoughts that I've been struggling with. I want to let go of my association with material things and while I am 75% there intellectually and physically, I am still not emotionally able to do so. I want to, and I know why I want to. I struggle with the fact that I like what options money can bring and what I can do for others with money. I like being able to fly first class and stay in nicer hotel rooms and treat friends to dinner or tip the barista $100 just because. I like these things. Part of me (and I'm not sure if it's ego-based) likes material things to a certain extent given their comforts. I also have huge goals for my businesses and goals of owning planes and other huge material things that I know won't bring me joy—maybe happiness, but that is short-lived.

I know that it's not the goal itself, it's the journey and who you have to become in order to achieve the goal—the level of consciousness I need to raise in order to achieve that goal. That every emotion anyone is looking for through a material goal, we have already achieved in our lives. I also know that success without fulfillment is the ultimate failure. So if life happens for us and not to us, how do I keep the goals of material things and goals for businesses without jeopardizing what is ultimately important in life: being?

To a certain extent, the reason why I was successful was ego-based. Now, I feel my "why" is to share a message and my own experiences, to create economic prosperity, and to create leaders who are not just wealthy economically, but wealthy physically, emotionally, with their time, relationships, and contributions. It seems that it is paradoxical at times.

Maybe I am thinking too hard and just need to feel more. When you get a moment, I'd be grateful to hear your thoughts.

Never give up,
Adam

Like all good mentors, he didn't give me an answer, but rather asked some powerful questions that continued to send me down the path of my spiritual journey, a journey I am still on.

And because I know I have a lot of successful business owners, leaders, and high performers reading this book, I'm sure that email sounded familiar. It is likely a question you are wrestling with as well: How do we keep the goals for material things and goals for our businesses top of mind without jeopardizing what is ultimately important in life: being?

That, my friends, is what the 200% life is all about. The beautiful thing is, we can have both! I've been on this journey for almost two decades. It takes time, and yet there will never actually be an "arrival." There are always new layers of your own spirituality to discover. Just like success is sequential, spirituality is sequential too.

Take heart! Your inward journey will not be easy, but it is simple (if you don't overthink and over complicate it).

Maharishi Mahesh Yogi, an Indian yoga teacher known for popularizing Transcendental Meditation, said,

> "All this message of the inner life and outer life is not new, the same age-old message of the Kingdom of Heaven within. 'First seek ye the Kingdom of God and all else will be added unto you.' It is the same age-old, centuries old message, but the message emphasizes today that it is easy for everyone. Without exception, born as man, every man has the right, the legitimate right to enjoy all glories that belong to him, all glories of the inner world and all glories of the outside world. And here is a process every man can directly experience for himself."

Maharishi was specifically referring to the Transcendental Meditation technique, which I practice, but that is only one of the ways to enjoy "all glories" of the inner and outer world.

I'm about to invite you on a journey of spiritual and personal growth. This is not a pass or fail test. There is no goal to achieve. No race to win. Keep your mind clear and your heart open. Everything will unfold exactly as it should at the right time for you.

2

In the Beginning

Every new beginning comes from some other beginning's end.

—Seneca

As we embark on the exploration of the 200% life, let's start by going back in time when the laws of nature ruled the world we live in.

One of the laws of nature is the law of cycles. Cycles are an inevitable part of our existence here on earth. From birth to death. From economic expansion to recession, to inflation, to depressions. There are times of quiet and rest, and other times of non-stop work and growth. Life is nothing but an ebb and flow of energy and experiences that we are lucky enough to be here to witness and enjoy.

I believe that over the past forty years, we have been operating in an elevated state of more, better, faster. How much could we accomplish? How much money could we make? How many things (cars, houses, watches, iPads, vacations, etc.) could we acquire? How many promotions could we get in just a few years? How many date nights could we go on? How many hours could we work and how little could we sleep? How many businesses could we start? How many employees could we hire? More was never enough.

Because of the "hustle hard and grind until you get what you want" mindset that has permeated our culture over the past several decades, we started to see some pushback from employees and people in general. This is why the whole "work-life balance" concept swept through the business world a few years back. Too many people were pushing too hard for too long, and for what?

Then March 2020 hit, and the world just paused. Most of us were forced to stop hustling in the traditional sense and reevaluate our lives and what was really important to us. In fact, the COVID-19 pandemic may have been the universe's way of forcing us all to pause, reflect, and reevaluate our lives.

So what has emerged a few years later? One thing that was solidified for me was that life wasn't about work-life balance at all… it wasn't even about work-life integration. The point is to be present in whatever part of my life I am in at that moment, what I like to call work-life presence.

Work-life balance is a myth… it's not a true reflection of life. It's impossible to keep your life in perfect equilibrium at all times.

In the *Tao Te Ching*, Lao Tzu writes about The Great Way, or the middle path, but it's not a linear line. It results from the action of moving back and forth between opposites. Move to one side too much, and you'll feel the pull to swing back to the other side. Go too far in one direction and you'll swing back just as far in the opposite direction. It's not like walking on a balance beam and hoping you don't fall off. It's more like skiing down a mountain with slight movements from side to side. The less extreme the swings, the more forward progress is made and the less energy is consumed doing it.

The *Tao Te Ching* was written in the 6th century, but the message is still completely applicable today, particularly when it comes to balancing our lives. We like to think that in our modern world, we are the only people struggling with these types of challenges, but it's amazing when you read texts like this to see how humans have been struggling (and suffering) in the same ways since the beginning of our existence. Just one of the cycles of nature, perhaps?

One hundred years ago, people worked to live. They enjoyed their leisure time. And just sitting around a campfire with a friend or family member was enough. Somehow over the years that changed to living to work. And I believe we are now shifting back in the other direction again. And with that, there have been a whole host of other workforce and business changes, such as more work-life integration techniques, employers supporting a more holistic work environment, conversations at work that are vulnerable and transparent, and the encouragement to show up as your whole self at work.

I think our society as a whole, not just the workforce, is looking for something more. We are at an interesting time in history where people are more willing to have deeper (and sometimes more controversial) conversations about spirituality while questioning and challenging their own beliefs.

Even just a few hundred years ago, these conversations were pretty commonplace. And if we look back a thousand years, spirituality, work, and life were all simply part of a person's everyday human experience. I think we, as a collective consciousness, are ready to embrace that state of being again.

KNOW THYSELF

As with most things, we can learn a lot from those who have come before us. The call to self-knowledge, as evidenced by the use of "know thyself" by the ancient Greeks and Egyptians, permeated their culture and shows just how much they were already in tune with their spiritual and inner world. As early as 2000 BCE, Egyptians adorned their burial sarcophagi with the phrase "know thyself." The ancient Egyptians believed that when they died, their spiritual body would continue to exist in an afterlife very similar to their living world.

Perhaps "know thyself" was a reminder that self-knowledge, whether in life or death, is the ultimate purpose.

The Greeks also inscribed "know thyself" on the forecourt of the Temple of Apollo at Delphi, which was completed in 327 BCE. Apollo's temple attracted a great diversity of worshipers because he was the god of virtually everything: sun and light, music and poetry, healing and plagues, prophecy and knowledge, order and beauty, archery and agriculture. Did the Greeks also want to keep the idea of self-knowledge front and center for all to see when they came to worship at the temple? I think so.

"Know thyself" appears in many cultures and traditions throughout history from Asia, to Africa, from Chinese dynasties to the Hindu teachings, to Islam, the Sufis, ancient Rome, and Eastern and Western Europe. Can "know thyself" be the ultimate and universal truth? It seems to transcend time, countries and cultures. And that is a powerful thing.

So, what's with the history lesson, you ask? When did this ultimate quest for self-knowledge, this 200% life existence, dissolve into self-indexed and external world-only living? It's hard to say. I think our Western culture has been more affected by it than perhaps other cultures. One can blame the industrial revolution, capitalism, consumerism, and a whole host of other things. It's no secret that our culture rewards people for going after what they want for the sole purpose of power and monetary gain. But it may be more simple than that. At some point, we just sort of lost our way and forgot that there was a whole other 100% of life available to us inside.

THE CROSS

The cross is a near-universal symbol of Christianity, a symbol we can learn much from. The cross in Christianity carries the message of love, finality, fulfilled promises, and it represents great sacrifice and the assurance of salvation.

However, the cross actually existed much earlier than that as a religious symbol rooted in ancient paganism. And before that, a cross-like symbol, called the Ankh, was one of the most recognizable symbols in ancient Egypt. While the meaning of the pre-Christian cross varied, several common themes centered on the intersection of the spiritual and physical worlds.

For example, the Ankh is an Egyptian hieroglyph for "life" or "breath of life." The Egyptians believed that human, or earthly, life was merely a part of eternal, or spiritual, life. The Ankh was a symbol for both human existence and the afterlife.

Some spiritual teachers believe that the cross represents the interactions of the divine (the vertical axis) and the human (the horizontal axis). At the intersection, the meeting point of the cross, you have the unity of the human and divine. It's where god (whatever "god" means to you) and the human experience collide.

I see the symbol of the cross much as spiritual teachers do. The vertical line represents the being part of you (spiritual), while the horizontal line represents the doing part of your life (physical). The intersection of the spiritual and physical is the 200% life.

The doing part of life is fun, challenging, and rewarding. It's how we propel ourselves forward to being a better "doer" of life. But if we take that same approach of searching, setting goals, and acquiring more on our path toward spiritual enlightenment, it doesn't work. If we set a goal to find enlightenment just to check it off our to-do list, then we've missed the point. You must call off the search and just *be* in order to find out who you really are.

ENTREPRENEURSHIP

It's interesting, too, what a journey entrepreneurship has taken over thousands of years. To us in the Western world, entrepreneurship seems like a concept that only emerged en masse in the past fifty years with household names like Steve Jobs (Apple), Bill Gates (Microsoft), Martha Stewart (Martha Stewart Living Ominmedia), Elon Musk (Tesla and SpaceX), Herb Kelleher (Southwest Airlines), Sara Blakely (Spanx), and Jeff Bezos (Amazon). Now, that is largely thanks to the media (and social media), and yet there is no denying that entrepreneurship is on the rise.

And yet, entrepreneurs existed in 17000 BCE in the form of traders and merchants. John-Baptiste Say, a French economist, coined the word "entrepreneur" around 1800. The word is taken from French, where it means "undertaker"—i.e., one who undertakes a new venture. And that's just what thousands of men and women have been doing for thousands of years: creating, innovating, and bringing those ideas, products, and services to the world.

In years past, you were either a man of the cloth or a man of the world. You were either a spiritual seeker or a selfish seeker of power and money. You either renounced all worldly pleasures or overindulged.

But isn't there a better way? A middle way?

Yes, I think so. And, the answer is the 200% life.

Business Meets Spirituality

Business is nothing but a conduit for your personal and spiritual growth.
                                        —Adam Hergenrother
                        (Yes, I just quoted myself in my own book.)

While on the surface it appears that business and spirituality (remember, we're talking about spirituality here, not religion), should be kept at arm's length, they are actually a great complement to each other.

What better way to grow spiritually and personally than to have to handle all of the challenges of working in a business, managing unhappy clients, making and managing large amounts of money, experiencing cash shortfalls, communicating with different (and sometimes difficult) personalities, hiring and firing people, navigating a global pandemic, and everything in between.

In this fast-paced, achievement-oriented, productivity-hacking world we live in, I think we've all forgotten how to just live and play and enjoy life. We grit our teeth, clench our fists, and hustle and grind until we burn out. We are stressed, anxious, overwhelmed, and uninspired. To what end?

I'll let you in on a little secret here… no one gets out alive! We're all going to die. We're only here for a very short period of time and we often take ourselves way too seriously. What if we just relaxed, released, and surrendered a little bit? What would life look like? How would it feel?

CAN BUSINESS AND SPIRITUALITY CO-EXIST?

I don't only think that business and spirituality can coexist, but that they *must* coexist. The business leaders of tomorrow are going to have to be just as concerned with their spiritual and inner growth as they are with the bottom line in order to thrive in our new global economy.

A decade ago, I don't think I would have been having these conversations, much less host a podcast and write a book about this very topic. Fifteen years ago, I had a very narrow definition of what business meant—it meant money, success, and significance, at least to me. And spirituality meant church on Christmas Eve or a celibate yogi living alone in a small house, meditation on a mountaintop, and renouncing money and worldly possessions. Business and spirituality were never in the same conversation.

Based on my belief of what spirituality meant, I knew that was not the life I wanted! So, when I was twenty-five, I ignored any thoughts of spirituality and set my aim on mastering the business world. And I wasn't looking to merely be moderately successful here; I was prepared to dominate anything and anyone I needed to in order to achieve my goals.

And dominate I did. In my first year in real estate, I was breaking sales records and winning both local and national awards. I had an assistant, built a lake house, and had a Hummer and Porsche parked in the garage. I had hit my "dream big" annual income number in just a few years and I wanted everyone to know.

So, at a holiday party at my mom's house, I told her I had made over $500,000 that year (of course loud enough for other family and friends to hear). She looked at me and said, "That's great, honey. Can you pass the ketchup?" She didn't care. My mom didn't value money in the same way I did (she still doesn't!). Her love for me and my worth in the family didn't depend on outside accolades or how much money was in my bank account. Her love was unconditional, so while she was proud of me, my external rewards didn't affect how she felt about me one way or the other.

That's when it hit me. If my mom didn't care, did anyone care? Did *I* even care? The money made no difference to how my mom felt about me, so why did it change how I felt? It was at this moment that I experienced a profound insight that money was never going to be the answer to whether or not I felt adequate or significant. I started questioning if there was more to life than money, material possessions, and recognition. I started wrestling with this idea and questioning everything. Money is money. Joy is joy. This pointed me towards a new path, a path of self-exploration and inner work.

As I started down this path, I wasn't quite sure what would happen to my business or my financial success. And to a certain degree, I was okay with that. I mean, there was a part of me, the ego, the lower self, that wasn't okay with it at all! But I knew that I didn't want to live a false life anymore. A life of chasing things to turn on my energy and make me feel okay, of thinking that a car, a house, or whatever would make me feel better permanently. That's false. It's not wrong, but it doesn't work.

So I became open to what showed up. Later that week, my wife, Sarah, gave me the gift of Transcendental Meditation for my birthday. I went to the introductory class right away and have been practicing it every day, twice a day for twenty minutes each session ever since.

From there I knew my real work was inner work, yet I still wanted to create and build in the outer world. I still wanted to play in business and sports and have children and experience all life has to offer, so I began to learn how to do both.

I felt pulled towards a path of using business as an opportunity to grow personally and spiritually. What if I could experience both? And what if I could teach others how to do that too?

BECOMING A FIERCE COMPETITOR

When spirituality and business collide, great things happen. When they coexist, the world gets emotionally intelligent conscious leaders who understand the importance of welcoming their employees' whole selves to work. We get authentic and productive employees who want to contribute to the company and beyond. We get companies that are just as conscious of humanity, the environment, and the world as they are about growth and profit. We get business professionals who can communicate with honesty, transparency, and vulnerability in order to get shit done without becoming attached to the outcome. We get a whole ecosystem of people who are clear, centered, and neutral and make decisions from this place of clarity.

Rather than pushing away spirituality and the exploration of the inner self because it's "too soft" for the business world or you believe that you may lose your edge, I would encourage you to reconsider. I would argue that spirituality and inner work makes you a fierce competitor in the business world. You are clear and conscious. Your decisions are not rash. You consider the ideas, feelings, and consequences of your decision before you direct others to act. You bring joy, enthusiasm, creativity, and energy to your work and to others around you.

If that doesn't create great employees and great companies, I don't know what does. I believe business *and* spirituality are the future. The path is in front of you. What will you choose?

Part Two
The 100% Internal World

4

Who Am I? Who Are You?

I am the Watcher. I am your guide through these vast new realities. Follow me, and dare to face the unknown, and ponder the question: what if?
— *The Watcher*, Season 1, Episode 1

Before we can really dive into this whole personal and spiritual growth thing, we need to talk about who is actually growing, who is surrendering, and who is experiencing the inner and outer world: the 200% life. We need to first understand who you are. The best, and perhaps easiest, place to start is by understanding who you are not.

You are not the voice inside your head. You are not your emotions and energy. And you are not the physical or external world. You—the You with a capital Y—are the one who is witnessing and experiencing all of those things.

First, let me ask you this, "Are You in there?" No one ever says no, and no one ever asks where "there" is. You just kind of know. Let's look at it another way. Make your mind say "hello" ten times in a row. Now, think of an apple. Did the apple that you saw bring any emotions up? Was it green or red? Who sees the apple? Who hears the voice? Who makes the voice say hello? That's YOU!

The very fact that you can use your mind to think a thought or ask a question means that You are not your thoughts or your mind. It is a subject-object relationship. You are able to use your mind as just another tool in your toolbox, much like you would a computer or your smartphone to help you navigate the world. The difference is that your mind is also mixed up with all of your personal life's experiences, not to mention that your mind is literally a part of your human body, which makes it that much more difficult to see the separation between the two.

Psychologist Robert Kegan, and author of *The Evolving Self*, explains the relationships we form throughout our lives as subject-object relationships. These start as the relationship between mother and child but eventually extend to relationships with friends, a partner, teachers, cars, houses, pets, clothes, coworkers, etc. In *The Evolving Self*, Kagan writes, "When the child is able to *have* his reflexes rather than *be* them, he stops thinking he causes the world to go dark when he closes his eyes." Before this understanding occurs, the child thinks that he/she is one with the parent and with the world around them. After the new awareness, the child has developed a subject-object relationship. And this is what we must remind ourselves of when we are talking about us versus our mind, emotions, body, etc.

Let's play out a scenario. If you happen to lose a leg in a car accident and I ask you if you are still there, of course you will say, "Yes, I'm still here." Clearly, you aren't your leg, you are the one experiencing the loss of a limb. Keep following me here. Let's say you had other complications from the car accident and it was recommended that you undergo additional surgery. The doctors keep you conscious and position a sheet so that you can't see what they are working on from the neck down. But, instead of working only on your leg like you thought, the doctors start operating on your hands, your arms, your feet, they even take out your heart and put it on a bypass machine. Your body is being kept alive by machines and modern medicine at this point. You aren't aware that any of this is happening. After most of your body has been removed, a nurse asks you if you're still doing alright. And your answer will likely be, "Yup, doing great." Then, of course, the second the nurse moves the sheet and you see what has happened to your body, your mind would begin to short-circuit, completely freaking out. You would be aware of the mind going crazy and you would also be aware that you have no limbs. I know this sounds like a B-rated horror movie, but this is an illustration of how you are, in fact, separate from both your mind and body.

Let's take one more example. Imagine you are ten years old and when you look into the mirror, you see a four-foot kid with a Ninja Turtle t-shirt and a mushroom haircut. Fast forward thirty years, and your body has grown and aged, and when you look in the mirror you see a six-foot-tall man with a few gray hairs, wearing a hoodie. That's just what the physical world does. It grows, it changes, it evolves. Everything and everyone is born, grows, and then dies.

But isn't it the same You today as it was when you were looking in the mirror thirty years ago, you're just seeing a different physical form? You are still You.

Why does it feel like you are your body? Why does it feel like you are the voice? Why does it feel like you are the emotions? When You, the one seeing and experiencing it all, are so connected to the ego, then you are unable to separate yourself enough to see that you are none of it. You are like the child before they had an understanding of subject-object relationships. While their understanding extends to things, people, and places, on your spiritual journey the objects begin to encompass everything from thoughts, emotions, and other energy patterns. You've taken it to a next level, but the concept is the same.

The following parable is another way to illustrate the hard-to-separate connection most of us feel to our mind and body.

Two young fish are swimming along. They happen to meet an older fish swimming the other way who nods at them and says, "Morning, boys. How's the water?" And the two young fish swim on for a bit, and then eventually one of them looks over at the other and goes, "What the hell is water?"

We are like the fish. We are so one with the water (our mind and bodies) that we can't see that we are in the water, but we aren't the water. Keep separating yourself from your mind and body and you start to see clearly that you are not them.

If you are still trying to grasp the concept of you versus your mind and body, don't worry, you are not alone! The difficult thing here is that until you experience it, it will be almost impossible to truly understand it. But I'll try to help guide you there. Here are two more examples for you.

A few months ago, my son, Asher (eight) was presenting in front of his entire school. As he was getting ready for the bus, he told me that he was nervous. Never one to miss a teaching or coaching opportunity, I said, "How do you know you're nervous?" Asher said it was because he could feel it. Then I replied, "Who feels it?" He said, "me." Of course, I kept the questions going and asked, "Who's me?" Asher said, "The soul." And that, my friends, is it. "I am the soul. I am the consciousness that experiences and sees." Our inner knowing is almost so simple that we overlook it!

When thinking about the separation of self from the physical world, I like to think of it like playing a video game—one of the very realistic ones like "Call of Duty" or "Ghost of Tsushima". I can see the human form, I can hear the voices, I see and feel the emotions, and I can touch all the objects. I have a big screen in front of me and I am watching it all unfold. I can toggle back and forth between zooming way out and seeing the entire landscape and all the people in it, or I can zoom in and focus on just one physical object. But I am the one who is in control. I am not the sword, or the building in the village, or the body armor, or the warrior. I am the one witnessing it all. As you continue to practice the subject-object relationship and move further and further back, you are able to be fully engaged with your inner world, while also fully aware of and engaged with the physical world (when you so choose). When you do this, you are living the 200% life.

For now, just remember that You sit behind all of it—the voice, the outside world, and your emotions. You are simply the one experiencing them.

So, when someone asks you, "Who are you?" you will answer, "I am the one who sees. I am the one who experiences all of life."

I AM THE WATCHER

If you've read this far, it's because you have questions that the mind is unable to answer. You have exhausted your intellect for the answers. You haven't been able to find them in the external world, either. And now you're stuck. The mind can't get you past this point. It has worked up to a certain point but, likely years ago, you started realizing that the mind is just not going to be able to scratch that itch. The itch is growing more and more annoying and persistent and you can't ignore it any longer. Congratulations. Now, you're ready.

All I want you to do right now is to start watching the mind trying to solve your problems. Not business problems or problems with your kids or finances. I mean, watch your mind try to solve the problem of this itch that you can't get rid of. Just observe. What do you see when you step back from the mind and watch?

You may be able to see that your mind is simply a tool that you have in your body, that you are in control of. Life and the world around you is unfolding, doing its thing, whether you like it or not and whether you are here or not (i.e., the weather, legislative changes, births and deaths, innovation, etc.). That's life's nature. Then there is the mind, which is nothing but a thought-generating machine. Energy is manifested in the form of yourself talking to yourself, which is what we call a thought. That's the mind's nature. There is the heart that has the same unmanifested energy that becomes manifested in the form of feelings. That's the heart's nature. And then there is the body that holds all of this together, much like how a car has an engine, seats, gas tank, and a steering wheel. All the parts come together to make the whole.

Then there is the driver of the car. The driver of the body. And that's You. You're only borrowing the car (your body) for a short period of time and getting used to all of the tools available to help you grow along the way.

When you see this separation and realize that you are the driver of the mind, the heart, and body, you experience an overwhelming sense of awareness that You are aware. You are here because you have growth to do. That growth is the evolution of your soul. The evolution of You!

Where do you go from here? You watch. Watch how many times your mind is wrong in an hour. Watch how your thoughts judge and contradict. Watch your heart vacillate between high and low vibrations throughout the day. Watch it all unfold. Go look out your window and watch life. Close your eyes and watch your inner life. Just watch. You are the watcher.

5

One Consciousness

You are not a drop in the ocean; you are the entire ocean in a drop.

—Rumi

As you start to see more and more of the separation between You and your mind, body, and the external world, a whole new phenomenon takes place. Eventually, you will move so far back behind the physical world and experience true separation, that you realize you are actually part of one whole consciousness! Yes, we have to separate in order to come back together, but in a totally new and different way.

Nothing is separate from the whole. And yet, everything arises from the whole.

Language is another construct of the mind. Sure, it's useful. It helps us categorize people, places, things, concepts, and ideas. It helps us communicate with others. It often gives us a sense of community and culture. But language has its limits. By the simple act of naming something, it cuts that idea or feeling off from everything else. Language and words can be a trap. They make everything seem separate instead of seeing and feeling everything as one.

Language, which is part of the human experience, categorizes, labels, and separates *everything*. The tree gets separated into roots, leaves, and branches. The town gets separated into houses, restaurants, parks, roads, and schools. The ocean is separated into waves, tides, trenches, seaweed, icebergs, and sharks. Yet each of these things is whole in and of itself. The ocean, the town, and the tree are a sum of all of their parts. A tree doesn't exist without sun and soil. So, isn't the tree also sun and soil? And the greater universe is a sum of it all.

You are the soul who has manifested from the one consciousness. We are all connected in this cosmic universe and you manifest as a human being in order to experience yourself. When you are part of the oneness, you are much like a drop of water in the ocean. Where does that drop begin and end? So, in order to experience yourself, duality and separation must exist. This is where the physical world comes into play.

Our soul uses the external world in order to feel more experiences and to continue to reach higher levels of consciousness. We can only move to higher levels of consciousness in the physical world, so we continue to come to this world to achieve that, which then allows us to achieve higher levels of consciousness in the spiritual world. And that, my friends, is ultimately who you are. A spiritual being having a temporary physical experience in order to achieve higher levels of consciousness.

Let's take a look at the path of the soul or spiritual being:

1. You are part of the infinite consciousness/oneness.
2. We separate ourselves from the oneness into an individual soul.
3. The soul enters the physical world in order to experience itself.
4. It takes us time to realize who we are in the physical world (we lose most of our memories of oneness once we move to the physical plane).

5. We leave clues (books, messages, children, drawings, buildings, etc.) in the physical world each time we are here in order to help us remember who we are the next time.

6. We reach higher states of consciousness as an individual and as a society, and we begin to remember who we are.

7. Once we move from "human doing" to "human being," we start rapidly evolving here on earth.

8. Higher states of consciousness in the physical world allow us to maintain higher levels of consciousness in the absolute world (oneness).

9. Our physical bodies die and our souls are returned to oneness until it's time to experience ourselves once again.

EXPRESS YOURSELF

Sounds so simple, doesn't it? Well, actually, if you really practice letting go and letting life unfold, nature and life itself will take care of a lot of this for you. No, that doesn't mean you just throw up your hands and do nothing! But it does mean you can relax a little and stop putting so much pressure on yourself. Believe me, life is way more fun this way.

So, if we know that we come to the physical world to experience ourselves, how do we do that? Usually, it is through some form of contribution or expression that we use to experience ourselves and remember who we are. Don't get lost in those words. I'm not asking you to raise one hundred million dollars for a charity or become a graffiti artist. But I am asking you to listen to yourself, the real You, to understand what speaks to you and pulls you towards action.

For me, it has always been business. Whether that was flipping cars or flipping condos in high school and college, or now owning several companies and brands. Entrepreneurship and business have been my main conduit for experiencing spiritual growth.

Building and growing a business forces us to look beyond ourselves; we've got employees, contractors, clients, and vendors all relying on us. We get to solve major challenges like layoffs and product delays. We get to create office spaces, social media posts, and technology solutions. We get to say the wrong things on a public stage and learn how to navigate lawsuits. We get to provide leadership coaching and training to employees and help clients buy their first home.

Business gives you all the highs and lows you would ever need to grow spiritually in this physical world. It's been the medium through which I have found I am able to express myself and experience myself in order to grow.

For others, expression and growth may come in the form of sports, parenthood, teaching, music, photography, interior design, or writing. The key to any *doing* is simply understanding what part of you is doing it.

The Four Phases of Spiritual Growth

Two roads diverged in a wood, and I—
I took the one less traveled by,
And that has made all the difference.
— Robert Frost, "The Road Not Taken"

Once you've decided to walk down the path of personal and spiritual growth, there is no turning back. While some people are naturally more centered and clear, just as some people are born with more athletic or artistic ability, the work is still the work. As your consciousness expands and new insights arise, it's impossible to go back to a previous level of thinking or knowing. You now have a deeper knowing, which means you will be different. But that doesn't mean you have to walk down that path alone.

There are four main stages of spiritual growth that you can use as signposts on your journey. Don't rush them. They will arise when you are ready, but it can be helpful to know what to expect. It also helps to understand what's happening once you move to each of the phases.

PHASE 1 - THE HONEYMOON PHASE

Imagine you just started dating your significant other. They don't care that you leave half empty cups of coffee all over the house, and you love them even though they are seven to twelve minutes late no matter what the occasion is. In other words, you are in the honeymoon phase. The honeymoon phase in a relationship is that initial stage of euphoria, happiness, and joy, where everything feels effortless and carefree. You're usually so emotionally high from the relationship that very little bothers you. Get fired from your job? It's okay—you're in love! Forget to pay a speeding ticket? No worries—you're in love! Stop returning calls from your family and friends for two months? It's fine—you're in love! Alright, you get the point.

A very similar phenomenon can happen when you start to really dive into your spiritual growth. At this point, you've likely discovered that all the material things, the money, the awards and achievements that are in the external world aren't giving you the same fuel and feelings that you had before. Your ego is starting to wake up and drive you towards more spiritual exploration. You may read a book that totally lights you up in ways you haven't experienced in years. You might begin a meditation practice that brings you peace and quiet. You have begun journaling, which provides a whole new level of calm and clarity in your life. You are loving this new feeling. It's the feeling you've been looking for. It feels really good and you want more. You've woken up and realized that there is more to life than the hustle of the external world.

You are right in the middle of the honeymoon phase and you're ready to devote your life to being a spiritual seeker. Well... at least your ego is.

PHASE 2 - REALITY SETS IN

The honeymoon phase can last for weeks, months, or even years for some people. It all depends on how far your spiritual ego takes you. If it's been all sunshine and rainbows, that may be a sign that you have some more work to do. Spiritual growth is hard. And it's easy to fall into the trap of spiritual bypass, which John Welwood, transpersonal psychotherapist, describes in his book *Toward a Psychology of Awakening* as a "tendency to use spiritual ideas and practices to sidestep or avoid facing unresolved emotional issues, psychological wounds, and unfinished developmental tasks." In short, it's the practice of taking a shortcut, which isn't really a shortcut at all! It may appease your ego, but it's not going to get you to the true spiritual growth you're after.

At some point, you'll just be driving along, listening to *The Untethered Soul* by Michael Singer for the twelfth time and a car in front of you will cut you off. And you will go off, honking your horn, throwing up your hands, cursing the day that other driver was born. Well, that's when you realize that the whole spiritual identity you've built for yourself is bullshit.

Reality sets in and sets in hard that you are really still at the beginning of this whole spirituality thing. You accept that you intellectually understand the spiritual growth concepts you've been studying, but you don't really feel them viscerally yet. You know the information in your mind, and can share it with others, but you haven't really experienced it for yourself. You haven't yet experienced that inner knowing.

This is when you have to make a choice. Do you want to stay on the spiritual surface or do you really want to dive in—even if you don't know what's going to happen?

I'm not saying that it's an easy choice. It took me many years to get there. About ten years ago (after a couple of years in that honeymoon phase), I realized that the purpose of my life was to let go of the part of me that was preventing me from fully experiencing and enjoying life. My purpose was to grow spiritually and leave this physical world unencumbered.

When reality sets in, you realize just how much further you have to go and, in fact, that the journey never ends. When reality sets in, you realize that your previous way of thinking doesn't work for you anymore. When reality sets in, you understand that you have to aim higher. That is inner growth and spiritual growth. You begin to see that there is a different way to live, that there is something bigger than yourself, and that all of your actions before were just to support the ego. When you aim higher, you see that truth. And that is where the path leads you next.

PHASE 3 - THE REAL WORK BEGINS

After reality sets in, the real work begins, and continues…and continues…and continues. This work will take a lifetime (maybe even a few lifetimes!). You now know that you have to set your aim on something higher than getting what you want and avoiding what you don't want.

If you are aiming at the physical world, then that's what you're going to hit. If you're focused on setting things up to get what you want, how you want it, in the physical world, then that's going to be the level that you play at. All your decisions are made and executed with the external world in mind.

If you are in Vermont and set your GPS on Florida, then you'll always be traveling to Florida. However, if you set your GPS on Costa Rica, then Florida just becomes something you move through. You don't even pay attention to it on the way to your destination. The same holds true for your life. If you set your sights on the fact that your meaning here on earth is to grow personally and create an inner world that is filled with peace, joy, creativity, and love, then it's like traveling past Florida (the physical world). It's just something that is on your way.

When you can get to this place inside, then the quality of your life ends up being determined by the quality of your inner state. Period. And then anything that happens in the outside world is merely secondary.

So what exactly is the "real" work? Well, it's everything we're talking about in this book. It's creating a spiritual practice that helps you pause, stay centered, contemplate the purpose of your life, and to keep your aim higher.

Let's take a look at a typical experience in the life of a human and see what the real work looks like.

Tom's alarm goes off at 5:03 a.m. (got to play tricks on the mind with those extra three minutes of sleep!). The voice in Tom's head immediately wakes up and starts going crazy. "I wonder what Bill is going to say to that email I sent last night. I need to post on Facebook before 9 a.m. Did anyone like my last post? Ugh, I don't want to work out this morning. I need to make breakfast and walk the dogs. That's going to take up too much time, so I won't have time to work out. I might have time this afternoon as long as I leave the office by 4. Is it my night to pick up the kids? Maybe Kayla can do it. She's going to be pissed; this is the third time I've asked this week. Flowers. That's it. Get flowers on the way home. Leave the office at 3:30 just in case. God, I can't wait until our vacation in Florida next month… piña coladas… I'm going to stop drinking alcohol until that trip. I better get up or I'm not going to have time to walk the dogs. Ah, Bill did respond. Looks like our pitch meeting is on for tomorrow. I'm not sure we're ready…."

And that is just within the first five minutes of waking up. Sounds fun, right? Don't worry, I won't leave Tom hanging. The first thing he needs to do when he's triggered by all of the details, worries, and anxieties of the day is to just play with the energy. Nothing is happening outside, he's not in Florida, he's not in his pitch meetings, nor is he walking the dog or working out. He can acknowledge that his mind is spinning itself up and start to diffuse that energy. He can talk to himself and simply remind himself that it's only the voice in his head talking, everything is fine. Affirmations or a mantra like "3, 2, 1… Relax" can work. Tom can meditate or simply get out of bed and walk out of the room. The goal here is to not make it worse. Don't buy into what your voice is saying. Acknowledge it. Diffuse it. And get back to center as quickly as possible.

There is no doubt that those thoughts and your voice are stirring up a lot of emotions and energy. It needs to be released in some way. Tom's typical modus operandi is to bottle up all of that energy and lash out at his wife with a snippy comment or lose his patience with his kids before work. He's not alone. Most people suppress their more negative emotions and then let them loose when they are in a "safe" environment, typically with people who are the closest to them. But Tom has been working on his spiritual growth and decides to do the more difficult thing: he acknowledges that he's got some negative energy building up and takes a time-out to meditate for five minutes.

By meditating, Tom is able to neutralize the energy. The energy doesn't go away, it's always there, but he took a pause and decided not to play or engage with the energy. After his meditation, Tom is able to go about his day, without unleashing any of that negativity on those around him.

Later in the day, at the office, Tom is hit with emails and calls from clients, several of whom weren't happy with the new pricing model. Tom was able to draw upon his "3, 2, 1… Relax" mantra each time this energy arose to bring him back to neutral. This neutral state allowed him to respond to his clients calmly, with clarity, and with a plan of action on how to move forward.

This is the real work. It doesn't end. It can become a bit easier or more natural over time. The time between disturbances may lessen. And sometimes the things that used to bother you, like a car cutting in front of you, don't even touch you any more. Of course, something else is bound to pop up. After all, we're having new experiences every day! But once you've started to incorporate the real work into your life, it's there for you to tap into whenever you need it.

All of this letting go sounds great, but how do you know what to do with yourself each day? What direction are you supposed to follow?

Follow me here for a minute. Life is kind of like a corn maze. We have a lot of corn mazes in Vermont, some of which take hours to get out of. Just when you thought you have found the exit, you come to a dead end and have to turn around and go back the way you came. The fastest and easiest way to get out of the corn maze is to orient yourself by climbing a ladder or way up on a hill to get above the maze. As soon as you are above, you can clearly see the way through. You know immediately which direction to travel, how far you are from the exit, etc.

When you rise above the worldly way of living you will see what direction you need to go.

PHASE 4 - TRUE SURRENDER TO IT ALL

Over time on your spiritual growth journey, you will stop touching and engaging with the energy and events that disturb you. It doesn't mean that you won't feel them, that they won't be extremely painful, or on the flip side, that they won't be completely euphoric. It simply means that you allow the event to move through you without touching it, pushing it away, or clinging to it.

You're no longer asking the mind to make you feel better. You don't need your mind to narrate the world around you or tell you that you are okay. When you truly surrender to life, you are the watcher. You witness the mind, you see the emotions, you see the heart move, you watch the external events unfold around you. You experience them all! Yet, you don't become attached to any of it.

When you truly surrender to it all, you've come full circle on your spiritual growth journey. But it's not a linear process. Spiritual growth is like a spiral staircase—you come full circle, while constantly leveling up. In essence, you've returned to the feelings of excitement, inspiration, and joy that you had during the honeymoon phase, but instead of your ego participating, it's You. The real You.

Another way to think of this is in terms of unconditional surrender. You are willing to surrender to all of life, no matter what may happen. You dance with it, interact with it, enhance it, but ultimately, you are surrendering to life. You get out of life's way so that you can interact fully with it.

True surrender also means that you don't necessarily get what you want. A true yogi would never want the world to give them what they want. They are already full and joyous inside. When you accept the events that are unfolding, you can bring your full self into the events.

We aren't talking about living a passive life or not taking action. Surrender doesn't mean inaction. In *The Bhagavad Gita*, thousands of years ago, Krishna said, "You have the right to perform your prescribed duties, but you are not entitled to the fruits of your action. Never consider yourself to be the cause of the results of your activities, nor be attached to inaction." Translation? Do your work, but let go of the outcome. Focus on the right action and let the rest unfold. Let go of the ego that feeds pride, significance, power, etc., by doing the work. And do not allow yourself to be tied to inaction. We are meant to contribute and work in the world.

You can have all the goals and experiences you want in life. Enjoy them all! What you are surrendering to is the fact that life is going to do its dance, always. It's going to unfold without your influence and control. You surrender the lower part of you, the part of you that has an issue with the event or what is being asked of you. Start with the little things, the rain, the driver in front of you, the fact that your avocados aren't ripe, or that there is no children's Tylenol in the store. When these things happen, the part of you that wanted it to be a certain way gets frustrated. That's the part that you surrender.

People think surrender is letting life kick your ass or something, but that's not it at all. It's surrendering to life so you can kick ass with life. It's not happening *to* you, it's happening *for* you. Remember you are a participant in life. You are experiencing life and life owes you nothing but the experience You are having.

True surrender is not hard; it's only hard when we compare it to how we think life should be.

The world has been here for 4.5 billion years. It took 4.5 billion years for you to be sitting exactly where you are right now reading this book. And you think about how it should be different!

There are millions of events and experiences that had to take place in order for this moment right now to happen. For example, a flight was canceled in the MidWest a hundred years ago due to residual effects from a storm in the Arctic which caused Sam and Joey to meet in a hotel while they waited for the next flight out. They stayed in touch and Joey introduced Sam to his sister. They had a child, but put them up for adoption. That child was your father and on and on. You're here because of a weather pattern in the Arctic decades ago! It's arrogant to think that we know how life should be. We don't know anything.

But our mind sure likes to try to convince us that we do.

7

The Voice in Your Head

The mind is a place where the soul goes to hide from the heart.
—Michael A. Singer

When I was in the early stages of my personal and spiritual growth journey, much of what I read and learned was about how to control my mind and change my mindset. I used positive affirmations, learned how to cultivate a mindset of abundance, and used hard exercise to quiet (well, really distract) my mind and build emotional fitness. And all of those techniques worked…until they didn't.

The mind is strong in its own way and will constantly fight against even your best intentions. It wants what it wants and what it wants is usually wrapped up in comfort and the path of least resistance. And that is no way for you to be able to grow and live fully.

The mind tends to live in the 100% outer world and you have to fight through it to get to the other 100% inner world.

THE PAIN OF INNER GROWTH

One of the hardest things you'll ever do in your life is to try and manipulate people, places, and things to match how you want them to be. It never works and the constant manipulation causes immense suffering. And who's doing the manipulating? That's right. Your mind.

You know what else is hard? Trying to fight with your own mind. Go ahead. Give it a try. Try to rebel against your mind. Try to fight it. Try to wipe it from existence. This is why some spiritual seekers go on hunger strikes or try to remove themselves from temptation or distraction. They are trying to get away from the mind. But it doesn't work.

You are human and therefore it is your nature to have a mind and an ego. All species on earth have their "hard." Ours just happens to be letting go of the ego and surrendering to life itself.

Sounds so easy doesn't it? Yet, not only is the path of inner growth painful, it's downright scary! We make a plan for our career and then we have twenty-eight contingency plans in case that first one goes wrong. All day, we're in our mind weighing the odds, playing through different scenarios, and guarding ourselves against an outcome that may or may not happen.

Why do we do this to ourselves? It's because our mind is trying to create the perfect scenario so that you will always be okay. You've built up all of these walls and constructs of the mind, just to avoid getting hurt. And then we wonder why we are nervous and anxious all the time. It's hard to hold it all together!

When we accept that spiritual growth is going to hurt, we can really get down to work. We can either have the pain of staying where we are in this constant battle with our mind, or we can have the pain of letting it go and growing spiritually. They are both difficult. But you get to choose which pain you want. And the choosing in itself is a form of acceptance, one way or another.

There is no doubt that people are looking for something "more" in their life in the form of personal and/or spiritual growth. But they want their version of spiritual growth—quick and painless. Real spiritual growth, though, is out of our control. It's messy and hard. It requires a deep surrender of the personal self. The hardest thing you will ever do in this life is work on yourself at this level.

As you move toward truly living a 200% life, you could upend everything you thought you knew, so it should not be surprising to hear that life will be harder. It may be that way for a while. Embrace it and enjoy the experience! Remember that you are not your mind, you are simply the one watching.

AWARENESS OF THE MIND

Right now you're reading this page or listening to this book and your mind is narrating what you are reading:

- Who is this Adam guy?
- I need to finish these five more pages and then check my email.
- What time do I need to pick up the kids today?
- What is this 200% life thing? I'm not sure I fully buy it.
- What's wrong with wanting and working hard for my dream car?
- Aren't I supposed to be mastering my mind?

But you are not actually the one narrating—that is your mind. You are the one watching and listening to your mind narrate what you are reading. The more we can work to separate ourselves from the mind and see it as a separate entity (part of us, but not all of us), the deeper we'll be able to go.

Awareness is such a key component of spiritual growth. Stay aware that you are not your mind.

Here's an example. You believe that you've really made some progress on letting go and accepting what is. You work on being more in alignment with your true nature. And you still like nice things in the external world! You appreciate your diamond ring and matching earrings. You finally bought your dream car, a Cadillac Escalade V-Series, all black with tinted windows. You feel great about your choices when you're alone. But when you get ready for the day, you question whether or not you should even wear the jewelry and have a ten minute conversation with yourself about the diamonds. And you get a little nervous pulling up to the carpool line in your Escalade and your voice starts going crazy. Instead of making these choices naturally and effortlessly, there is a whole battle going on inside your mind because of what other people may think. This is just the voice, it's not You!

Or how about when you are up for a promotion at work and you catch wind of your competition. Your mind starts rapid-firing thoughts about why you are better than them, why you deserve the promotion and they don't, how they have performed poorly over the last quarter, and the fact that you've saved their ass more than once. This is just the voice in your head, it's not you!

The aforementioned are both perfect examples of your mind having a *mind* experience instead of *You* actually having an experience. When you're listening to the voice, you're not enjoying your jewelry or your car or the opportunity to interview for a promotion or the people around you. You're stuck in your head with that incessant chatter.

I bet you're wondering how to get rid of that voice, aren't you? I mean, why is the voice always talking? Well, if you're human, and you're alive, then you're going to have thoughts. That is just part of the human experience. The mind's nature is to produce thoughts. A sky's nature is to have clouds, stars, and the sun. A wolf's nature is to howl. A tree's nature is to shed its leaves during fall. We don't ask why, it's just the nature of it.

One way to start embracing the separation between yourself and the mind is by naming the voice in your head. My kids call their voice Johnny. By naming your mind, you create a clear separation between you and your voice. Then, when that annoying little roommate in your mind (aka Johnny or Jasmine or Jake) starts acting up, you can call it out. Acknowledge that Johnny has a pretty loud opinion, but it's just that—an opinion. You can ask Johnny to be quiet, or you can ignore Johnny all together. An ignored guest quickly leaves. And then you can be back to experiencing the moment without your mind running interference.

YOUR MIND IS A TOOL

Every fall for as long as I can remember, I take some time to go hunting. More often than not, I'm there for the experience of living simply for a week or so. Limited cell phone service. Non-existent WiFi. Just a couple of people communing with nature. My favorite part of these week-long hunting trips is the solitude and the hours of time and space to just be.

Inevitably, at some point, my mind will begin to wander and I start to think about my thoughts, what they mean, how to let go, and surrender and rise above it all. All while trying to call in an elk from 300 yards away.

But thinking will only get you so far in life. In fact, it generally prevents you from fully engaging with life and the events that are unfolding around you. If I'm thinking about something that's happening back at the office, while I'm physically at a family barbeque, well, then I'm really in the office in Vermont, and might as well have stayed home.

I'm not saying don't think or use your mind! Your mind is a very useful tool, but it's just that, a tool. It's not you. Your mind produces thoughts. Your ego narrates the thoughts and decides what to pay attention to.

You are in the moment because you're using your mind to create your life, or at least your mind's interpretation of life. The problem is when you use your mind to escape the moment and go back to the past or think about the future. It's not real, those are just thoughts. The only thing that is real is this moment right now.

But using your mind to solve problems in the present or using your mind right now to plan for the future is what it was designed for. We have a very highly complex and skilled mind at our disposal. There is nothing wrong with consciously using the mind to have conversations, solve problems, make connections, and plan for the future. You are in control of your mind. Do not let it control you.

When I'm hunting and scanning the trees, I work to be aware of my thoughts instead of allowing them to take over and go in a million different directions. I might consciously decide to use my mind during this quiet, uninterrupted time to work through a difficult business problem and play out different scenarios.

Another way to use the mind to your advantage is succinctly put in the common phrase "mind over matter." When people say mind over matter, they are using their mind to overcome a physical or emotional challenge. You are willfully using your mind to solve a problem. I used this technique a lot when I was competing in Ironman races. It usually was in the form of a mantra or positive affirmation, and yes, sometimes just playing mind games with myself! During particularly tough moments of the triathlons, I would tell myself, "Run to the next aid station," or "Just bike to that next tree. You can make it to the top of the hill." I created a way to override the mind so that it didn't talk me into quitting. Which it tried to do! The mind is tricky like that. The key here is that I used the mind as a tool to keep me going. I did not let that voice inside my head take over. I knew I was not the mind, and therefore was able to use it to my advantage. And you can too.

STOP PLAYING MIND GAMES

Alright, so you've started by accepting that it is your mind's nature to produce thoughts. Some are relevant and some are irrelevant, and there is everything in between. Ninety-five percent of our thoughts show up spontaneously. They aren't deep insights or life-changing epiphanies; usually they are just low vibrational thoughts. No big deal. It's only a problem when we start to attach ourselves to them.

Now, this doesn't mean you're indifferent to the thoughts. It just means you are looking at them and seeing them for what they are: nothing more, nothing less.

What you do with the thoughts matters, not whether or not you have thoughts.

I like to think of this like babysitting our thoughts and emotions. Most of us are going around "babysitting" and tending to our thoughts on a minute-by-minute basis. We are engaged with them, playing defense, reacting to them, trying to control them, and attempting to make them (the thoughts and your mind) okay. But this is no way to live! You don't want to be constantly babysitting your mind. If you do, you have no reprieve and no separation from your thoughts, which means you have no space to work on you—to work on watching and experiencing the thoughts rather than becoming attached to them and then "babysitting" them.

When a thought arises, just say, "Okay, it's a thought." But if you follow the thought down the road and tie a rope to it, that's the problem. The mind never sits still and never behaves. It just keeps wanting to win, wanting to make your ego safe and secure and it will do anything to accomplish that goal. It's a ridiculous game and it causes so much unnecessary suffering.

People think they understand what spirituality is and what going on a spiritual journey will entail. But they put conditions on it. They will go on a spiritual quest, but only if they can keep their money and material possessions. They're up for a spiritual awakening, but only if they can maintain their same identity as the "go-to problem-solving extraordinaire" for their family and as a leader in the community. True spiritual growth has no conditions. You are not going to know what's going to happen until it happens. You have to be willing to let go of the outcome.

This unconditional spiritual growth means that you stop playing the game of the mind. You stay in the world, you engage with the world, heck, you even play the game sometimes, but *you* are not the game. You have separated yourself from your mind and can see when the game is being played. It's a losing battle to try to get the world the way we need it to be in order to feel okay, so stop trying! If you play with the energy at the level of the mind, you will always be living in the mind, and never really living at all. Relax, accept, and release.

I know, I know… easier said than done.

Moving From Your Head to Your Heart

The Spiritual path is the disciplined inner journey from the ego to Soul.

—Lyna Jones

Remember, what you do with your thoughts matters, not whether or not you have thoughts in the first place. Thoughts are inevitable.

Every day your brain processes over 6,000 thoughts. How many of those are actually helpful, useful, constructive, positive, or even interesting? Why do we allow those thoughts and our mind to rule our lives?

The same is true for all the events happening in the world. Ninety-nine percent of events that unfold around you move right through you—someone else's kid being late for school, your neighbor getting a new dog, or your coworker breaking up with their partner. These are all events, but they just don't touch you or trigger you. But then, we all have those things that just set us off, like a long line at Starbucks, running out of eggs, your cell phone battery dying.

The events around us and our thoughts are inextricably linked. So, that's where we will begin with letting go.

The next time one of these small events disturbs you, just stop and allow yourself to sit and feel the disturbance, which is all part of the beauty of the heart. Don't push it away. Don't go to your mind to try to make it better. Just sit and allow that feeling to move through you. And it will. Now you are one step closer to realizing that you can handle anything. It is a constant practice and does get easier over time. You will find that peace is just on the other side of allowing events to move through you.

When you begin to move from your head (the mind, your thoughts) to your heart (your soul), you are shifting your consciousness. You move away from trying to understand language and thoughts and life to *knowing* life, instead.

Your insights are already inside you and when you stop paying attention to the mind, you can turn your light instead onto your insights and let them shine through. The energy, light, and love that we are looking for is already inside of us. In Luke 17:21 KJV, Jesus said, "... behold, the kingdom of God is within you." What we are looking for has been inside of us all along and it is through this spiritual work and letting go of listening to our minds that we can begin to experience life from a different place. Spirituality isn't about changing what you do, it's about changing what part of you is doing it.

THINKING TO KNOWING

Your mind is great at what it is designed to do: produce thoughts. Your mind is a thought-generating machine. Sure, it can solve problems and make decisions too, but what if I told you there was another way to achieve the same result?

In *The Most Important Thing*, Adyashanti writes,

"Ingesting other people's answers is safe. It doesn't

challenge us all that much. It doesn't force us to dig deep within ourselves. It doesn't force us to find our own revelation. It just provides a ready-made answer. Even if that answer is about as close as words can come to providing an answer. It's still not yours until you actually perceive it and experience it. It's still not yours. It's somebody else's. It doesn't belong to you until you experience it for yourself. Until you know whether it's true or false for yourself."

You can intellectually understand everything I am talking about in this book. You can start to bring awareness to this new state of consciousness. You can start to have glimpses and moments of surrender and begin to raise your consciousness. But it's in the experience (not the knowledge) that will lead to truth. And once you experience it, it is yours.

Think about the last time you attended a business summit or online masterclass. You get hours and hours of expert advice, inspiring information, and fresh ideas. Great! But until you actually put any of what you learned into practice and experience what it feels like to make a new hire, take control of your calendar, or decide to shut down one of your divisions, it's not really your experience to own and learn from. I'm not saying *not* to read books, attend conferences, or listen to podcasts. They definitely fast-track people to a new level of awareness. But until you put the information you learned into action, then you won't really change your business, your life, or your spiritual self.

Knowing is the way you tap into your inner self and your inner wisdom. It's that deeper inner voice that is in alignment with your true nature and tells you what is right and wrong *for you*. When you operate from this place of knowing, not just thinking, life moves you in the direction that you are meant to go.

9

Keep Your Heart Open

Power is influence over external events.
Peace is influence over internal events.

—James Clear

Now that we have started to explore the mind and the voice inside your head, it's time to take a look at the heart, which is where your feelings, emotions, and energy emanate from. When you move out of your head and into your heart, you continue to move deeper down the path of your spiritual journey.

The 200% life requires you to accept that there is a time and place for the mind and thoughts and the external world, and there is a time and place for our energy, emotions, heart and the internal world. Eventually, you will have peace and the inner world will be your constant, and you will dip in and out of the external world as you choose.

THE HEART

Do you feel your heart? Maybe, maybe not. If you've just gone on a really tough run or are nervous before a big meeting, you may feel your heart beating. But most of the time, it's doing its thing and we're not even paying any attention to it.

But have you ever had that physical sensation of your heart dropping? Like when you answer the phone and you know there is some bad news on the other end. Or when your partner of twenty-five years asks for a divorce? Your heart just drops. But, it's not like your heart actually moved.

On the other hand, have you ever felt your heart spontaneously fill up with joy? Like when you get that call that your adoption application has been accepted or you made partner at your firm. So what exactly happens? Your physical heart is likely still beating, your heart rate may or may not increase, but either way, you feel different. That's what I will be referring to when I talk about "the heart." The spiritual heart, not the physical heart.

Just like your mind is what hears your voice and your thoughts, your heart is what feels your emotions and energy. It's the spiritual conduit for the energy in your life.

The heart is very ethereal. It's like the wind. Impossible to pin down, and easily changed and moved. One second there is a light, warm breeze and the next, the wind can kick up and start blowing leaves and bending trees. Your emotions, like the wind, can shift quickly and take you over.

Let's go back to that sensation of your heart dropping. When you start to feel the heart, what most people do is go to their mind to hide from the heart (i.e., the feelings and emotions), because they can't handle the emotions that are emanating from the heart.

You've probably felt this more often than you think. Here's an example. You're in a meeting with potential clients and you're working through your very thorough and well-rehearsed presentation. When you pause to take a breath, your colleague jumps in and starts taking over. Your heart drops. You knew this was going to happen, but it had been going so well! You're frustrated, disappointed, and embarrassed.

Your mind jumps in to "save" you and your mind starts telling you that it's okay, it doesn't matter who closes the deal as long as it's done. But why does she always do this? Who does she think she is? Oh well, she's better at presenting than you are, anyway. You contributed the whole plan, and they know that. It's fine. Keep smiling. The pitch is almost over.

As soon as you go to your mind, you start to close your heart. You go to the mind, because you know you can tell the mind to make you feel better. The mind always agrees and starts leading you down a path of chattering about why the event shouldn't have happened, why the other person sucks, how much better you are, why you shouldn't get your hopes up, and on and on. Your mind is tricky like that and, for the most part, we are glad our mind "protects" us!

Too often, we get caught up in the extremes of our emotions. If we feel good and our heart rises, we want to chase after whatever causes us to feel that way. Conversely, if our heart drops, we get scared and want to push away and hide even more from that low vibrational feeling. Either way, these intense feelings trigger people (i.e., the consciousness) to hide. This becomes a natural protective mechanism that people use to avoid feeling the full range of the heart, including pain, joy, or other emotions. Buddhists refer to this as pushing away an experience.

But when we hide from our emotions, we are unable to truly experience the heart for what it is. It's what 99% of people do and it's no way to experience life!

What would life be like without a heart (no, not the physical heart, but the spiritual heart that allows us to feel)? It would be a pretty empty existence. There would be no depth to life. The problem is that most people want to control the spiritual heart so they close their heart before the real emotion or energy hits.

As difficult as it is, if you can keep your heart open, then you never need to go to your mind to make everything okay. When you keep your heart open, you start to fully experience life. We are designed to feel it all! The highs, the lows, and everything in between.

But remember, that doesn't mean we need to get caught up in our emotions. They are just events that occur. You must understand that you aren't really controlling any of the processes of your heart or your mind. It's just unfolding in a natural process. The events come in, your heart feels something, then your mind comes into play and does its thing. You have zero control over this cycle. Your heart moves involuntarily, your mind starts talking without any prompting from you, and your dreams just pop up however they want to. It's just a process. So we let the process do whatever it needs to and we take up a witnessing position. We relax and release behind it.

Over time, the process doesn't have a hold on us. We just understand that it's happening. It's like watching the weather do its natural thing—it rains, it snows, it's hot, it's humid, there's a rainbow, and the clouds shift, the sun comes out, then the moon rises. We witness it all and don't judge it or become personally attached to it.

The heart is one of the greatest gifts given to the human experience. It gives us a richness and depth to life. But we know that doesn't mean it is always open and flowing. Sometimes our heart becomes blocked with stored energy and emotions that can begin to negatively influence the way we interact with the world.

SAMSKARAS

When an event (such as a thought, action, or emotion—all of which are just energy) can't make its way through us, then it becomes stored. But, energy must move, even if it's blocked. So, these stored energy patterns take the form of a circle so the energy can remain in one spot, yet continue to move. The energy wants to get out, but we won't let it. These are called samskaras.

Samskara is an ancient Sanskrit word. I like Yogapedia's definition of samskaras:

"Samskaras are the subtle mental impressions left by all thoughts, intentions and actions that an individual has ever experienced. Often likened to grooves in the mind, they can be considered as psychological or emotional imprints that contribute to the formation of behavioral patterns. Samskaras are below the level of normal consciousness and are said to be the root of all impulses, character traits and innate dispositions."

The powerful energy creates a mental impression—a samskara—which has a tremendous amount of energy stored within it. Think about how many events in your life that you haven't let go through you, positive or negative. It's not just the negative or painful energy patterns like a breakup or losing out on a job opportunity that are stored. It is the positive ones too, like your child's first birthday, the day you bought your first home, or when you made your first $100,000. You either clung to or pushed away the energy. Either way, it became stored as a samskara, and most of us have many more negative than positive samskaras. Even the positive ones can eventually have negative effects when we use them to compare every other experience to previous ones and start constructing all sorts of expectations and preferences for the way life should be.

Each samskara has different levels of energy within them, which is why some events feel worse than others. You are energy and you have a vibrational code, as I like to call it. And every event has a vibrational code to it. Each vibrational code has a different feel to it that you experience. An event such as losing money feels different than when you make money. We then decide which vibrational codes we like and don't like, hence a samskara is born. When the energy is trying to come up and be released, it hits your stored energy (your samskara) and creates a vibration that we experience as anger, frustration, jealousy, etc. These samskaras have effectively blocked you and cut you off from the energy that is naturally flowing through you.

You can think of your natural energy like the water in a beautiful flowing river. If you start to add boulders and rocks to the river, the water is going to have to navigate around the boulders to make its way through. If you keep adding more boulders and rocks, eventually only a trickle of water will be able to make its way through. Now, you've blocked the river. You've blocked your energy.

So, what are we to do with all of these samskaras? Well, what most of us do is go to the mind and ask the mind to figure out how to make us feel better. By feel better, I mean to feel the juice of life that is within us, that natural energy flow that has been blocked. And the mind always has an answer. The mind says, "Great. I think you should go buy a new car, and while you're at it, why don't you skip your workout, grab a bottle of wine and a pizza and treat yourself. You deserve it and you'll feel better." And because we are addicted to the mind, and all of the ways the mind takes away our pain, we agree. We thank the mind and go buy the car.

But this is a false and fleeting way to achieve the true feelings that we are after. We attempt to change the external world in order to not have to deal with the samskaras. It works—for a while. Maybe a few weeks or months. But, eventually, that energy high starts to fade. And instead of getting rid of the energy blockage, we go right back to the mind to solve the problem. We want another energy high and the mind has another answer for us. We have the car, so now the mind tells us we need to propose to our girlfriend and get a puppy. If only we had that, everything would be okay. A few weeks later, that energy has faded and we're back to the mind again looking for something more to make us feel okay. It's a vicious cycle of us trying to get things from the outside world to make us feel okay inside.

The only way to remove a samskara is by allowing the samskara to work its way through you. In order to work its way through you, the real You needs to relax and allow the event, the energy, to move through. Once it's moved through you, it's gone forever. That's the greatest gift. It's very painful and you will feel that pain when you're releasing it. You never try to manipulate the emotion or the event, you simply relax and allow the energy to work its way through you. There is no shortcut here. The minute you touch the energy, you're right back in it. You're now fighting with the event and it's almost impossible at that time to let it work through you.

Think of a samskara as a dead skunk in your fridge. Every day you come home and the house reeks. You get some Febreze, you open the windows, and clean the rest of the house, but you won't get near the refrigerator. Sometimes the smell goes away, right after you clean, but you're always worried about coming home, smelling the skunk, and having to deal with it. You've thought about selling your house just to get away from the smell. The dead skunk is running your life! You play this game over and over for years.

Yet, if you want the smell to be gone, all you need to do is go over to the refrigerator and remove the skunk. Easier said than done, because you know that as soon as you open the fridge door, the smell is going to be worse than it ever was before. The smell will be so intense until you've removed the skunk from the house. But once it's out, it's out. That's what will happen when allowing a samskara to move through you. When it's gone, it's gone.

The minute you can relax long enough to let the event go, the samskara burns up forever. But to be clear, it will be painful, which is why you have resisted it so much in the first place. However, as painful as it might be, once it's gone, that samskara is gone for good.

It's important to acknowledge your samskaras and do the inner work described throughout this book to allow the samskaras to move through you. Why, you might ask? Yes, it will help you live a more centered and peaceful inner life, but let's not forget the other 100% of our life! When samskaras are removed, you become a more fulfilled and focused leader, you run your business with more empathy and effectiveness, and you build relationships based on true connection and understanding. In short, you become a fierce competitor in business and life, while still maintaining your inner peace.

10

Everything Is Energy

Being fully human is not about feeling happy, it's about feeling everything.
                                                    —Glennon Doyle

After exploring some of the more difficult stored energy patterns through the lens of samskaras, let's shift gears to how we navigate energy, emotions, and feelings on a daily basis.

We all know those people who are ruled by their emotions. One minute they are overcome with joy and pride when they get a promotion and a raise at work. The next moment they are frustrated, angry, and resentful when they hear that their colleague also received a pay raise, but $1,000 more a year. The excitement they felt was almost immediately replaced with anger and jealousy. And worst yet, they acted on it by passively aggressively congratulating their colleague and then leaving the office early. We've all been there. I know I have!

But there is a better way to live and move through life. I'm not asking you to eliminate any of your emotions. Emotions are part of being human. However, we can create a more neutral energy inside ourselves instead of jumping on the emotional rollercoaster and going for a wild ride.

What most of us do when an emotion shows up is that we begin to wrestle with it. We start talking ourselves out of the emotion, good or bad. If we are really excited about an upcoming vacation, we may start to tell ourselves, "Oh, don't get too excited. The airlines are a mess right now, we'll probably get delayed. Don't get your hopes up too much. Noah may not actually propose on this trip, he's probably waiting until New Year's Eve." And the inner monologue goes on and on. The same is true when even more negative emotions arise. You begin to fight the anger with something like, "I was right to get angry. He didn't deliver the report on time and that made me look bad. He's got to learn. Maybe I shouldn't have said what I said in that tone, but I was still right to tell him what he did wrong." And that inner monologue continues. Either way, we wrestle with positive emotions or negative emotions. It's like throwing a rock into a pond. And then jumping in afterwards to try to smooth out the ripples. We all know that doesn't work. It just makes a bigger disruption and more ripples!

If the ripples are our emotions, here's what we can do. After a ripple (emotion) has been created, instead of jumping in after it, do nothing but watch. Just watch the ripple or emotion. And what happens after a little bit of time? It goes away! And you didn't have to get wet or expend any energy. Most of us spend our whole lives trying to smooth out the ripples. Some of us have even gone so far as to move away from any pond that has any rocks within a mile so that no one can ever even throw a rock in. But instead of avoiding the inevitable emotions, accept them and watch. Remember, you are not the emotions; you are the one watching and experiencing them.

Energy is a more holistic word to describe our feelings and emotions. An event is just energy. In fact, everything is energy! Our bodies, our thoughts, our feelings, our cars, our cell phones, our pets, the food we eat, the universe. It's all energy. Sometimes the energy and vibrations are very dense and we see objects like chairs, our hand, a computer. Other times the energy is less dense and invisible to the naked eye, such as light, emotions, sound, or thoughts. We innately know that everything is energy, though quantum physics gave us scientific evidence. Turns out science and spirituality are a lot more closely aligned than one may have thought.

Alright, so we know that emotions are just energy. We have simply given them words to help us better categorize and communicate the very minor differences in energy patterns. For example, you have an inner knowing of the subtle differences between anger and irritation, between hurt and anger, between happiness and joy, or between frustration and disappointment.

Let's look at a specific example. When you lose a loved one, the energy from that loss is extremely painful. You don't want to experience that feeling again, so you may go through your life protecting yourself from getting close to another person so that you don't get hurt again. On the other hand, you may even bring up that feeling of loss again and again and stay stuck in it. Neither one allows you to truly operate as the highest version of yourself.

Larger events like death, a failed business, or divorce may take longer to move through you. Most people will try to push that event away, choosing to not experience the event fully. What happens next is that the difficult event becomes stored as a vibrational energy pattern inside (a samskara). And because it is now stored, we continue to relive and feel the same energy pattern over and over again, sometimes for our whole lives!

Now, there is nothing wrong with feeling the emotion. Again, we're humans, emotions are going to happen! But we don't need to "live" in that emotion or dwell on it. It's okay to feel the emotion as long as the event that is sparking that emotion is actually happening. If one of your parents just died, of course you'll feel it. It may take weeks or months to allow that event to fully make its way through you. But a clear being is able to experience the deepest depths of the heart and emotions (yes, it will be painful and deep) and still allow the energy pattern to make its way through them.

Think of events like a storm. Some storm cells rain for an hour and then the fog and mist lingers for a few minutes after the rain shower. It's damp and your patio furniture is wet, but within a few minutes, the sun comes out again and everything dries up. This is like a tough email you got from a client or some feedback from your boss that triggered your feelings of self-doubt.

However, if a hurricane comes through your town, it may last what seems like days, wreaking havoc on businesses and the landscape, and displacing people from their homes. The effects of the hurricane are much more devastating and it can take a while for the sun to come out and for the town to be cleaned up. This is like experiencing a death, breakup, bankruptcy, or losing your job.

Each storm (event) definitely feels different. In each case, the key here is that you relax and release. If you relax and release every time the event is felt (right after it has occurred), you are wiping down a wet chair or picking up debris from the hurricane. Each time you do this, there is less work remaining for you to clean up so that you can return to that neutral state—that seat of self—faster and with less effort.

The same is true for events that you don't like that are happening inside of you, such as frustration, anger, or unhappiness. You think they are happening inside of you, because you may not be able to point to a specific external event that is making you feel a certain way. Regardless, what is happening inside of you is typically a direct reflection of something that is happening outside that you are resisting in some way. You have a certain expectation for how you should feel and when you don't, you experience an internal energy shift that may be negative, restless, uneasy, angry, etc. If there is a negative energy shift, something is causing it.

What we humans typically do is try to find an answer, either on

Google, with our friends, or a therapist. We want to know what is causing this shift so we can protect ourselves from it in the future. That is not a bad first step; there can be some useful information there. And, of course, there may be times when one will only find healing through therapy.

However, I've found that all you really have to do is sit with the shifted energy pattern. You actually don't need to figure out what is causing it at all! Allow the negative feeling to arise through you and let it go. Don't go to the mind to analyze it. Let go of trying to solve the problem. Just let it go. Once you realize you're the one holding the feeling down, it becomes easier to allow it to make its way through you. Let go of the feeling of "needing" to know the root of the issue before letting go. It really doesn't matter at all, as long as you let go of it.

If you stay on this journey long enough, at some point, even if a hurricane comes around, it will move through you as fast as it arrived, leaving zero debris. It's cleaned up at the exact same moment that you experience it.

Where we get caught is in the push and pull of the energy and emotions. If it's an event or feeling we really like, then we cling to it. If it's an event or feeling that we don't like or don't want, then we push it away. But there is a sweet spot where you acknowledge and accept the event and emotion that comes with it, and then allow it to pass through you—no pushing, no clinging.

When I get hit by a particularly strong emotion, I like to remind myself that if it's not happening outside, then it's not happening inside. Take memories as an example. We can use our mind to recall something that happened in the past, but then we attach emotions to it and label the memory "good" or "bad." We do this so much so that we can begin to have physical reactions to the energy we are recalling along with the memory. But the memory isn't actually happening, so we don't want to get caught up in thinking that energy/emotion is happening inside. We can watch and observe the memory, but we don't have to become attached to it. Too often we end up living in the past or future and miss the moment right in front of us because of our deep attachments to our emotions. And when we live in the past and future, we are living in the mind and are missing out on all the actual experiences of life happening right now!

After all, your mind never wants to be left out! It's going to insert itself into every area of your life that it can.

Your mind creates a mirage that you get to watch and then you wait to see if you like the feeling enough to take action on the image that your mind created. You end up assessing all of your options and making decisions based on feelings of some future event that may occur—future events that your mind conjured up!

This is how desire works. You think about a new house and instantly you start to feel better. Your mind manipulated the energy inside of you to give you a taste of what it would feel like to own a new home. But it's a future event. It's not real. It's a mirage. And it doesn't work. You only go after things because you think you'll get that feeling that the mind created with thoughts and images and encouraged you to go after it.

What if you stopped and asked yourself, why don't I just feel this way all the time? Why do I need to desire something (or get something) in order to feel this way? Why can't I just feel this level of happiness and fullness first, without the mind game, and then go play in the external world?

If you stop and contemplate these questions, what you'll realize is that you think the mind, the egoic or personal mind, is your best friend. You think it's the gatekeeper to your energy flow and that it controls all you are looking to get out of life. But that couldn't be further from the truth.

The reason you don't feel the energy flow is because of the mind in the first place. It's like you're in a rear naked choke hold and you're gasping for air. Then all of a sudden you ask your mind for help and your mind obliges and you're able to get your opponent to release their grip so you are able to breathe. You thank your mind for helping you get out of that suffering, only to find out that your mind had you in the rear naked choke all along.

The mind wants you to need it in order to feel emotions and energy, but you don't need it at all. You don't need to ask the mind for anything. You can experience the full energy flow all the time and for no reason (that you can point to in the external world). That's real spiritual flow.

I want you to think about the most amount of energy that has ever flowed through your body. Maybe your first intimate moment, the birth of a child, the first $5,000 cash you earned, a kiss. Whatever it is, think about how high your energy felt at that time, think about how much energy was rushing higher and faster than it does during your everyday life.

If you're not sure whether or not you have that energy stored inside, consider this: Remember the first time someone broke up with you? Your energy was so low mentally, spiritually, and physically that it was hard to walk the dog, call your dad back, or want to do anything but watch hours of *Survivor*. And then, all of a sudden, your ex sends you a text message that says, "I love you. I miss you. I'm coming over." How much energy just miraculously sweeps through your body? You immediately move, jumping in the shower, shutting off *Survivor*, and smiling from ear to ear. So, what happened? Where does this energy come from? Was it the text? Your ex didn't give you anything. Your cell phone didn't inject you with some sort of energy cocktail.

Nope. You just opened your heart back up! It was just good, old fashioned energy stores, opening up and bringing you peace, joy, and happiness. You felt the highest rush of energy that you've ever felt. And that's only about a one on a scale of 1–100 in terms of the energy that you can feel every minute. A one! When you're at a negative fourteen most of the time, getting to a one feels fantastic.

What if your starting point every day was a one? That's the goal, for me anyway.

Every night I fall asleep knowing that part of me is gone forever. I didn't store any new energy patterns. I kept my heart open. That way, I can keep increasing the flow of energy within me. That's all I'm concerned about. Letting go so that I am fed from within. My energy inside fuels me.

For more than half of my life, I wanted to feel good, so I would go outside myself to be fed in order to feel a certain way. But when we are fed from within, there is no reason to look to the external world for validation. When we are untethered from the outer world, we are free. And when we are free, we interact with the external world in a completely different (and joyful) way.

11

Die Before You Die

The ego is always looking to find something—the spirit can see what's already there.

—Marianne Willamson

One of the human conditions we have to navigate in order to let go of the outer world and be free is the ego.

When we think about ego, we often think about someone who is arrogant, who has an elevated sense of self, or who is overly confident. The most common definition of "ego" is a person's sense of self-esteem or self-importance. In short, when we talk about ego, it's usually not in positive terms! But the ego is more than that. Our egos are the personal identities that we have created. And our minds are always working on trying to protect our egos.

However, there is a different way. If we really want to achieve absolute freedom in our lives, then we have to stop trying to protect the ego—and instead, let go of it altogether.

WHAT IS THE EGO?

So much of what we experience are just impartial, neutral events; they aren't personal. Think about how many things happen every single day. Around 385,000 babies are born each day around the world, and about 164,000 people die each day. Businesses are started from laptops, and major corporations file bankruptcy resulting in mass layoffs. A glass shatters at a restaurant in Helsinki, and a surfer catches a wave in Hawaii. A star falls from the sky and hits the Earth's atmosphere, and an egg falls out of a bird's nest. Do any of these events affect you or bother you? No!

There are billions of events that happen every minute that you are totally unaware of and unaffected by. So, it can't be the event itself that is the problem or the thing that is causing you suffering.

But then why do we make everything personal? It's a very human thing for us to do. Is that just how we are hardwired? Kind of. The Earth has been in existence for 4.5 billion years, yet homo sapiens (humans) have only been around for about 300,000 years. That's not very long in the grand scheme of the universe. Part of the human process and experience right now, based on our evolutionary stage, is the fact that we developed an ego.

And your ego is part of your psyche. Think of your psyche like a house. The house has bedrooms, a kitchen, a back deck, an office, a dining room. Just like a house, your psyche encompasses all the inner workings such as the mind, thoughts, emotions. Your ego is the entity that lives inside that house and moves from room to room slamming doors, leaving the lights on, starting fires, opening windows. The ego is the transient part of the psyche that moves within it and uses different parts of the psyche to get you to pay attention to it. The ego uses thoughts and emotions as a way to feed itself and generate energy.

Essentially, our ego is a part of the mind that collects past experiences (maybe even from other lives), including things we've read, people we've met, or ideas we've learned, and used those to create a personal identity. By the way, that identity is just a fictitious character you and your ego have made up. It's not actually you. You are the one who created it and are witnessing it. And, that also means that you are the one who can release it and remove it.

Somewhere between three and five years old, humans begin to develop the ego. While we begin to understand that this is a subject-object relationship between ourselves and everything around us, the "us" is still a personal identity (an ego) at this point. At some point in the evolution of homo sapiens, perhaps the ego goes away, but right now it is part of the human experience.

We can see the evolution of, and perhaps the emergence of, the ego in humans through the story of the Garden of Eden and the fall of Adam and Eve. Let's put a specific religious interpretation aside for now, and consider the allegorical principles one can find within the story. Here's the short version:

> Adam and Eve were happily living in the Garden of Eden, innocent, naked, and in an egoless state of consciousness. They were created by God in his image and to live in union with God's divine life. Adam was tasked with maintaining the garden. His only other instruction was to not eat from the Tree of Knowledge of Good and Evil, because if he did, he would die.
>
> Enter the serpent, who convinces Eve that she will, in fact, not die from eating from the Tree of Knowledge. She will actually be able to understand good vs. evil and be like the gods. Of course, she eats from the tree and then convinces Adam to do the same. Their eyes are opened and they become ashamed of their nakedness. They fashion fig leaves to cover their bodies. God appears walking in the garden and Adam and Eve immediately hide.
>
> God calls out for Adam. Adam tells God that he

hid because he was naked. God asks Adam who told him he was naked and quickly suspects that Adam ate from the Tree of Knowledge from which he was forbidden. Adam blames Eve. Eve blames the serpent. Consequences ensue.

So, what is this allegory telling us about the ego? Adam and Eve were originally one with God, nature and their consciousness. By eating the forbidden fruit, they developed human knowledge with a focus on the needs of the bodily and psychological "self." Bryce Haymond, of thymindoman.com, offers a great explanation of the fall and the development of the ego:

> "Egoic self-consciousness, or an extreme heightened sense of self-awareness, seeks to protect its "self" at all costs and build it up as much as possible, to fulfill its most grandiose desires, and completely avoiding what it doesn't like, even seeking to destroy what it doesn't like. This "self" became the first priority of the human being. It wasn't enough to simply seek, eat, and enjoy the fruit of nature, but our "self" had to have the best, tastiest, most beautiful, most abundant, most extravagant foods that we could develop. And this kind of egotism extended into every area of human interest, to clothes, to housing, to social relationships, to experiences, etc. Our "self" became the priority in our lives."

That is what happened to Adam and Eve, and what has happened to the rest of the human population at this time. Regardless of how you believe the personal identity (i.e., the ego) was created, we now have a personal side to us. The ego operates front and center in our lives, until we commit to doing the deep inner work to move beyond it and back to that "oneness" with God, the universe, the infinite, whatever word makes sense to you.

As we become more aware of our ego, we begin fighting against it. But your ego won't give up easily!

Our first reaction in most situations is to respond in whatever way we think will get us what we want. And then once we get what we want, now we need to protect it and ourselves in order to maintain the identity that we created around that lake house, that promotion to the C-Suite, that influencer status, that Ironman athlete, etc. We all do it.

The ego wants to stay in control. It loves to get what it wants and it loves to be right. However, when the ego does get what it wants, it suspends itself for a few days or minutes and you experience simply what is (joy, pleasure, etc.). But the ego can't accept that for long, so it jumps back in and finds its hold. For example, you're on a great vacation and just as you sink into the feeling of being in the moment, your ego starts to tell you that it could be better—you could have gotten a room with an ocean view, the concierge could have given you a complimentary bottle of wine, and if only it wasn't going to rain tomorrow. Your ego likes to be heard and will crash any party, vacation, or mundane moment in your day if you let it.

Think about when we say things like, "I don't mind that he's late again," or, "Would you mind if I took the day off tomorrow?" On the surface, it sounds like we're good, everything's cool, neutral, we're tiptoeing into a conversation and everything's fine. But if we go deeper, what we are really doing is asking our mind to appease the ego. We aren't just saying, "I don't mind." We're telling (or sometimes asking) ourselves if the thoughts and emotions from someone being late or disappointing someone by taking a day off will be something that we can handle. We say it as a statement, but it's more like a rhetorical question. We're just checking in with the ego and asking the mind if it will be okay or not, and then our answer is determined by whether or not your mind will freak out or if it will be okay.

As I said before, this is no way to live and no way to become untethered and live a life of absolute freedom. Instead, we must surrender and let go of the ego.

DIE BEFORE YOU DIE

Eckhart Tolle said, "The secret of life is to 'die before you die'." This is not a modern-day concept. To "die before you die" is an age-old idea that has roots in Islam, Sufism, and other religions. Essentially, to "die before you die" means you achieve self-liberation and become free from worldly concerns. You also release attachment to the ego, while still living in this physical life. In short, your ego needs to die before you can really live.

When the ego smells its death, it will do *anything* it can to hold on.

The ego is a crafty shape-shifter. It will do anything it can to get you to pay attention to it. So, when it feels you starting to let it go, it knows death is imminent. The ego will then create a problem or start in with endless chatter to get you to put your energy towards it. It may even take on another shape in the form of a new goal or idea, in order to keep you engaged. The ego is adaptable, moldable, and flexible. For instance, if you love money, but then you renounce money in an effort to fight against the ego, the renunciation itself is just another form of the personal mind/personal identity (aka the ego) taking a different position. Or, perhaps you are motivated by power, but then you realize that power isn't what you are really after, so your ego tells you to go be a spiritual teacher. And then you end up creating a new identity as a spiritual teacher, all the while your ego is laughing at having tricked you yet again.

Just watch your own mind. The ego is fueled by your energy and attention. It switches its answers or opinions constantly. One day your favorite color is red, then you read a book, and the next day your favorite color is blue. But it will switch right back to red if it serves its purpose of protecting your identity or helping you create a new one. The ego's entire existence is based upon you paying attention to it. So it takes all the data and information you have stored in your mind and through your past experiences and tries to put together a compelling story about why when you do X, you will feel good. Again, it's like your ego has you in a headlock and is asking you, "Do you want to know how good of a friend I am?" Then it lets you out of the headlock and you think it's the greatest thing in the world. But your "friend," the ego, had you in its grip all along.

The ego creates problems, then wants you to give your energy to it. Then the ego miraculously solves the problem that it created. You then become dependent on the ego to help you live your life, make you feel good, to solve your problems, or help you make decisions. But it's all smoke and mirrors!

It is natural to want to fight against your ego, to try to talk it down, or resist its pull. Instead, I want you to ignore it. If you ignore the ego, there would be no problems! Don't pay any attention to your ego. Sure, you can notice it, but do not be pulled in. Acknowledge it and then look away. Awareness is the way out. Do not get entangled by giving it any of your energy—that's what it wants. But without your energy, your ego will be one step closer to being gone for good.

The End of Suffering

The Great Way is not difficult for those who have no preferences. When love and hate are both absent, everything becomes clear and undisguised. Make the smallest distinction, however, and heaven and earth are set infinitely apart. If you wish to see the truth, then hold no opinions for, or against, anything.

—Seng T'san, "The Hsin Hsin Ming"

If we must die before we die (i.e., let go of the ego) so we can continue down the path of the 200% life, then we must look at all of suffering too.

As Seng-T'san, the third patriarch of Zen, wrote in "The Hsin Hsin Ming," if The Great Way (a.k.a life) is not difficult for those who have no preferences, then it's safe to say that preferences are the cause of all suffering. At least Buddha thought so. One of Buddha's Four Noble Truths says that attachment to desire (preferences) causes suffering.

I'm not about to disagree with the Buddha, but it is a bit more nuanced than that.

THE CAUSE OF ALL SUFFERING

Let's take a look at this in action. Every year my family and I take a week-long vacation during the kids' winter break. We live in Vermont, so usually we pack up in January and head somewhere warm (the Bahamas are a family favorite). Now, you can imagine that flying with three kids and three adults (my mom always joins us) is difficult enough. But add in the fact that there are no direct flights from Vermont to Nassau, plus having to schlep the various recreational clothes and gear we bring, as well as the electronics for the eight-hour travel day... suffice it to say, it's not easy. Thank god we don't need the car seats anymore! No complaints here, just stating the facts of a family trip. I'm grateful that we are able to do this each year, that's for sure!

Logistics aside, I also have a few preferences. I prefer first class. I like an aisle seat. I like endless refills of seltzer water. I would like to leave on time and not be delayed or miss our connecting flight. In fact, I expect the airline to get me where I need to go on time. I prefer that there aren't any cranky babies on the plane and I like a turbulence-free flight. I expect my kids to behave and get along with each other throughout the day. And I expect to be able to answer my emails while in the air so I can switch focus from work to pure family time by the time we reach our destination.

In the grand scheme of things, these are pretty minor preferences and expectations. They sound pretty common for most travelers. Yet, we all know travel does not adhere to our preferences or expectations— like, at all!

But what do most people do? Stress out. Complain. Project their anxiety onto fellow passengers. Be rude to flight attendants and airline staff. Worry. Overthink. Yell at their kids. Suffer.

Fundamentally, the issue isn't with the preferences per se. Preferences themselves are just fine. The trouble we get into is when we attach ourselves to our preferences and allow them to dictate how we feel, how we act, and how we treat others. In short, allowing preferences to run our life.

We generally look at the world in four ways:

1. When we get what we want, we are okay.
2. When we avoid what we don't want, we are okay.
3. When we don't get what we want, we're not okay.
4. When we get what we are trying to avoid, we're not okay.

Long story short? We are constantly trying to manipulate and arrange the world so that we are always okay! We are always looking for ways to get the external world to match what we like or keep us away from what we dislike. Then we get trapped into playing that game for the rest of our lives, always looking for something in the external world to turn us on.

The reason why preferences are dangerous is that they end up controlling all of our actions. We start putting so much time and energy into our preferences (what we want to happen or don't want to happen) that they become the focus of our lives, instead of just experiencing life itself!

When we have a preference, we go after it and suffer along the way. We worry about getting it, we worry about what will happen if we don't get it, and then we worry about how we are going to keep it once we do get it. It's exhausting! And it just doesn't work.

Again, preferences themselves are not the problem. It's what happens when your preference doesn't come to fruition. Do you relax behind the energy and let it pass through you? Or do you get attached to not being okay and get caught up in the disturbance?

Now do you see why the Buddha said preferences are the cause of all suffering?

While I'll talk about the cause of suffering in terms of preferences and expectations, Buddhists often refer to desire, craving, attachment to the desire, or conversely, an aversion to something. Regardless of what words we use here, the point is that when we have likes and dislikes, and the world doesn't match up to those likes and dislikes, we suffer. Even the action of going after something we like or trying to avoid something we don't like is a preference, which comes out of disturbed energy.

THE PRESENCE OF SUFFERING

When we talk about suffering, we are not just referring to big events like losing a loved one or going bankrupt. In fact, when we talk about suffering, we're really talking about the every day change in energy that causes a negative feeling. Someone cuts you off in traffic. You get pissed. You suffer. You've been at work since 7:00 a.m. and your employee doesn't show up at 7:30 a.m. even though you never told them your expectations. Now you're angry that they didn't read your mind. You suffer. Your flight to the Bahamas gets delayed. You tell the flight attendant that this is bullshit. You suffer. And you cause everyone around you to suffer too! Suffering happens anytime your energy shifts and you allow it to take you over.

Unfortunately, humans are all about their likes, dislikes, and preferences. It is basically how we categorize the world. I like the mountains, I don't like the beach. I like seltzer water, but I don't like orange vanilla seltzer. I like dogs, but I'm not really a cat person. Actually, I only like hypoallergenic dogs, and dislike pretty much any other dog that's not my own. I like keeping my truck spotless, but I don't like doing the dishes. Honestly, the list goes on and on.

Let's really break it down for a minute. Imagine you're sitting on a rock in the woods and a snake slithers by near you. You see the snake and you immediately have a jolt of energy telling you that you don't like it. You can't believe that snake got so close to you and you instantly start pushing the experience away. Your mind then jumps in and starts narrating how awful the experience with the snake is, so you get even more tense and nervous, and start to push that experience away even harder. Objectively, nothing happened. Your mind was making up a whole story and you didn't allow the experience to move its way through you. You didn't accept the event for what it was. You just pushed the experience away and categorized the snake as a "dislike."

Now, a minute later, you get up from the rock and walk down the trail and a butterfly lands on your arm. It's beautiful; you can't believe it actually landed on you! You're in awe of the butterfly's beauty and light touch. You are loving this experience and can't wait to tell your kids about it. You hold onto and cling to this event. Just like the snake, you didn't allow this experience to move its way through you. You didn't accept the event for what it was. Instead, you clung to the experience and categorized the butterfly as a "like."

Now your mind says, "I don't like snakes. I like butterflies." In both cases, the experience never moved through you and because you pushed one event away and clung to the other, you are no longer neutral. You now have a preference for how life should be. Snakes: no. Butterflies: yes. Oh, and by the way, all moments should have butterflies because it will make you happy and you'll avoid any hiking trail, camping spot, or lake where you may encounter a snake in the future. These energy patterns and preferences that get stored are those samskaras we talked about in depth in Chapter 9.

We spend so much of our time trying to get the world exactly like we want it, based on previous experiences. Because most human lives are experienced from the egoic state of mind, we are basically passing judgment on what we like and don't like, what we want and don't want, every moment—and these judgements are mostly in our mind. It's so ingrained in our psyches that we don't even notice it happening most of the time. We are so addicted to the mind that we become oblivious to the fact that our preferences are running (some might say ruining) our lives. If, at any time, you are not aware of your thoughts, feelings, or reality, you have lost. You are unconscious.

Often people are able to get their lives organized just so, and they do feel relatively okay. And they think, "I'm not suffering." But I will challenge that. Do they feel ecstasy pouring through their body every moment so that all they have to do is close their eyes because the energy inside is so strong and joyous? If you're not operating from that state, then you're suffering. Sure, you may be suffering a lot less than other people, but suffering is relative, and you're missing the point. Any time you go after what you want or are trying to avoid what you don't want, you suffer. There is a fuller, more peaceful, and more joyful way to live.

THE END OF SUFFERING

Eckhart Tolle said, "For most people, their spiritual teacher is their suffering. Because eventually the suffering brings about awakening." A spiritual awakening is when an individual's ego transcends their ordinary, finite sense of self to encompass a wider, infinite sense of truth or reality. Simply put, you've moved further back enough in your conscious awareness to understand that you are part of the infinite oneness.

Why is this important? Because when we "wake up," we end suffering. And when you end suffering, it will then lead to more clarity in your life, your business, and your relationships. It will allow you to solve problems faster and either return to, or maintain, a state of neutrality more effortlessly.

How do we end this suffering, you ask? We stop having preferences and expectations!

Okay, now you might be wondering, what's so bad about preferences and expectations? Don't preferences point us toward our true nature? If we like one thing (maybe marketing) and don't like something else (like finance), aren't those natural signposts to help guide us to make decisions about our career and, ultimately, our life? How do you know the difference between a preference and alignment with your true nature?

This is a very deep conversation and the mind won't ever agree (pause and see how disturbed the mind is simply by reading this). I mean, of course we like and dislike things? What's wrong with that!?

Stay with me here. We need to create a very large separation from the mind in order to even see what is going on at this level. That's why every day, every minute you can work on this. Become aware of the mind, knowing that it is not you, letting go of the personal, getting clear and centered, and then acting.

At some point (usually the 4th Phase of Spiritual Growth), you will come to realize that there is another way to live. You will be able to look at a car, a tree, a person, a house, whatever and have no preferences attached to the object you are seeing. It's not bothering you. It just is what it is.

We know that all emotions are different energy vibrations presenting themselves in different ways. And your ego will always have a preference and expectation. It will always have an opinion. Its purpose is to create thoughts and steer you towards what it perceives as pleasurable and steer you away from what it thinks will cause you pain. The key is to stay vigilant. Pay attention and recognize what part of yourself is feeling these preferences. Acknowledge it and move on.

As you reach this phase, following your nature becomes much easier. The "aha" moments you experience are really just You—the real you—having insights that guide you towards what you are supposed to do next. It takes some time to be able to clear out the voice in your mind to be able to truly hear your heart. There is a deeper, more intuitive voice that will begin to show up and pull you. Right now, it's just so covered up with preferences, and samskaras, and your mind's chatter that it's hard to hear!

Ultimately, your preferences will pull you away from your true self if you allow them to. This is what makes enlightenment so difficult. You have to let go of your ego first, and your ego is a formidable opponent! But the beautiful thing is, once you get rid of all of the noise of your likes and dislikes, you will actually have space to find out what you're really meant to do. Instead of looking for things to fulfill you, you find fulfillment within yourself (with no external influences) and then you bring that fulfillment to everything you do in the external world.

That intuitive, inner voice is a pull toward what's true, while the preferences are purely of the mind. One is a mechanism of letting go (inner voice) and the other (the mind) is a mechanism of control.

IT'S HANDLED

It's tempting to want to rewire our likes and dislikes to move more quickly down the spiritual path. But that only works on the surface. If you just keep telling yourself that you don't like money and that you love volunteering at a local animal shelter, you're still living in the mind. Sure, you can flip how you view something by using your mind. It's a tool, after all. But a better way to approach the event in front of you is by acknowledging it, accepting that it's happening (you're not hitting your financial goals or volunteering at the shelter is wreaking havoc on your allergies), and know that you can handle it.

Acceptance doesn't mean that you don't take action. It means you take *clear* action.

Just last week my phone was blowing up. I had three different business leaders bringing me slightly different information, yet I needed to make a decision within the next few hours so that we could all move forward with clarity. I could have responded with exasperation, blame, anger, or confusion. Instead, I used one of my go-to phrases: "I'll handle it," or occasionally I'll say, "It's handled."

Did I have an answer? Nope. Did I have any idea how I was going to handle it? No, I didn't. But I knew I could. What would the alternative be? Getting spun up and emotional? Releasing that emotion on all of my employees and business partners? What good would that do?

You might not like it, but you are choosing to accept and handle whatever the situation is.

On the other side of the voice and the preferences is freedom. You will experience true freedom when you no longer need to see things through the lens of likes and dislikes and when you stop trying to arrange the world to serve your personal needs. Remember, you will still be interacting with the external world. You'll go to work, get married, run, play with your kids, and lean into life, but you're no longer manipulating the outside world to serve you. You're not even doing it for other people. You're just interacting with the flow of life. When preferences and expectations go away, you end suffering, and the world opens up and you become naturally aligned with your true self.

Part Three

The 100% External World

Need Nothing and Enjoy Everything

The meaning of life is just to be alive. It is so plain and so obvious and so simple. And yet, everybody rushes around in a great panic as if it were necessary to achieve something beyond themselves.

—Alan Watts

What would happen if we stopped chasing preferences, expectations, money, a relationship, the "right" job, the "perfect" body, or a successful business? Do those things really bring us fulfillment and joy? And if they do, how long will it last?

In November 2020, Tony Hsieh, the visionary business leader and former CEO of Zappos, died from smoke inhalation complications following a house fire in Connecticut. This was an unfortunate and tragic loss of a young life who had made significant contributions to software development, ecommerce, developing communities (he donated more that $350 million to rebuild Las Vegas), and to company cultures and the client experience with his book, *Delivering Happiness*. From the outside looking in, he had checked all of the boxes of what a successful life should look like. He seemed to have it all. But what Hsieh didn't have was a sound relationship with himself.

Friends of Hsieh said that he had been coping with mental health issues, heavy drinking, and addiction, especially in the year leading up to his death. He surrounded himself with "yes men" who were consequently on his payroll; their only job was to "be happy."

We'll never know everything that Hsieh was feeling and experiencing in his life, but his story shows us that no matter how great money and success can be, it will never give you a better relationship with yourself. But focusing on creating a solid relationship with yourself (the inner work) first will lead to having an amazing outer life. And it can be more effortless than you may think.

THE ART OF BEING VS. DOING

People think they have so much more power and control than they really do. There are so many things that occur in the natural world without any human involvement. Our hearts beat. Leaves fall off trees in the fall. The clouds change shape. Tadpoles grow into frogs. We unconsciously move our arms when walking. Who is making any of this happen? It's involuntary and spontaneous. It just is. We don't usually think too much about any of it, unless we break our arm or have a condition that weakens our heart. Only then do we have to grab a tool—our mind—to help heal, move, or do things differently.

Being is when you are completely present and in harmony with the moment. You are not trying to change or control anything. Instead of trying to "do life," you are just enjoying life.

The term "human being" says it all. We are not human doings or human doers. We are human beings!

First be and then do.

We surrender to the natural world all the time. We have an expectation (and probably take for granted) that it will all work as it's supposed to.

We've actually already surrendered to about 99% of life. But when it comes to what we want? Well, that 1% packs a powerful punch and is a completely different story!

It's not a bad thing to play with the human form and "do" things in life. The key is not to go after those things first but, rather, second. If you have an abundance of money, become a steward of that capital and use it wisely. If you find yourself in a leadership position or position of power, use your influence for good, and never at someone else's expense. If you find yourself on a unique and exciting vacation, enjoy all the emotions that come with the novelty of the experience! Just experience all of those things (i.e. money, leadership, power, travel) and don't become attached to them.

You are a human being first, who then goes out into the world and expresses your authentic self. It's the being world that is free of judgment, full of unconditional love, joy, and enthusiasm, and has very high states of consciousness. If you focus on this first, then when you enter the human doing world, you do so from a place of self-expression, joy, creativity, and contribution, instead of a place of need and want. You know when you are in the presence of these types of individuals. You feel seen, heard, and understood. You feel their generosity of spirit, kindness, and non-judgement.

So, yes! Go play and accomplish and do in the world. Enjoy the taste, the richness, and the vibrant experiences of life. But focus on *being* first. Being whole and complete inside. Being at peace. Being calm and neutral and clear. Being fulfilled and joyful. Being okay with everything.

When you approach life like this, you are truly being fed from within. That means you are not looking for anything in the outside world to give you energy. You already have a well of energy inside of you that you can tap into. You can access that well of energy whenever you want—you don't need a vacation, a promotion, or a certain number in your bank account for it to show up.

Imagine if that rush of energy was a constant source in your life and your starting position for everything that you did? Anything else you did in the external world would just be a bonus!

It is never about changing what you do, you simply change what part of you is doing it. Know *who* is experiencing the richness of life. Is it You? Or is it the mind or ego? It's a subtle shift in how you approach life. But it is life-changing.

SURRENDER TO LIFE

Not too long ago, we had a great question from one of our The 200% Life podcast listeners. I'll paraphrase, but essentially he wrote:

> "A few years ago, I maxed out $30,000 on a credit card and had nearly nothing in savings and the anxiety around 'what if' scenarios were real. Now having quite a bit of money in the bank, I don't have the same fear around not being able to provide for my family or fear of the 'oh shit!' moment if something goes wrong. And I think that does change the quality of life and happiness. Do you disagree?"

I think this is such a real and common example of how most of us feel about money. When we have it, we are happy and relatively unafraid. When we don't have it or don't have what we consider enough, we are unhappy and operating from fear. But, there is another way to play in this 200% life!

Here's how I replied:

> "Yup, the anxiety can certainly feel real, but even the $30K debt and 'what if' scenarios are still an imagined event in your mind causing you suffering. You can have

$30K in debt and figure out actionable plans on how to pay it off and you can address your spending, and do it all with acceptance of your present situation. Or, you can have $30K in debt and have a tremendous amount of stress and suffering because you are scared of what might happen and you may make poor decisions based on this fear.

But if something does happen (which is unlikely), you can accept it and then fight like hell to get out of it. Fighting like hell to get out of a situation is completely different than fighting like hell to get out of a situation because you think solving the situation will bring you joy and happiness. Once you get out of the situation, the debt, and feel happy again, you'll just find another thing to be happy or scared about. The cycle then continues."

The listener wasn't done with me yet! He asked:

"So it is just when you evolve internally that the stress no longer exists and the joy is more apparent? I definitely don't have stress anxiety around money like I used to."

Note: He doesn't have stress or anxiety around money like he used to because he has what he considers is "enough." If that changed, without the inner work, the stress and anxiety would return.

I answered:

"There is a real sense that you can lose stress when debt is gone. No doubt about that. It's relative, but it's real. You can improve your external situation to get your life relatively okay, however, if you don't work on the internal aspect of money, no matter how much you have you'll always have some level of suffering. Yes, paying off debt will lower your stress, because your stress is tied to something external. When you can point to why you have stress or why you have happiness from something outside yourself, you are still relying on the external world way too much."

As I mentioned above, acceptance or surrender doesn't mean that you don't take action. Surrender is not passivity. You can still fight like hell to change your situation to make it better. But just know that changing the outside world will never truly give you what you are after inside. As in the aforementioned example, paying off debt is a temporary fix to some deeper inner work that needs to happen.

I've had several moments of surrender throughout my life, but I'll share two significant ones with you here.

When I was in high school, I was 100 pounds overweight, failing classes, and experimenting with recreational drugs. One day I came home from school and was just overcome with this deep energy that told me that there was a different path for me. It wasn't a thought that generated from my mind. I wasn't thinking about anything specific other than my homework that was due the next day. This feeling moved me to take action and change the direction of my life, which I did. I surrendered to this inner knowing (though I didn't know that's what I was doing at the time). I cut out my "friends" who were no longer serving me, I lost 100 pounds, became the captain of the football team, and started focusing on my school work. It didn't happen overnight. It took a lot of work to get there. But it only took that one inner experience for a shift, an awakening, to begin.

That's all it takes. Just a shift in perspective. An inner movement towards a different path. Clarity that allows for greater truth.

More recently, I experienced another moment of surrender that I didn't see coming (but that's usually how it happens!). My family and I had just purchased about fifty acres of land, engaged an architect, poured a foundation, and had begun to build our rustic modern dream estate. Turns out, though, it wasn't the dream I was meant to follow! Within a few months of starting construction, my family and I kept finding ourselves in Stowe, Vermont. Stowe is only about forty-five minutes from the town where we were building our new home and where my kids go to school, but any free afternoon and on the weekends, we would head down to our little mountain house to hang out and do all the outdoor activities. About a week before school started, my kids asked, "Why can't we live in Stowe?" Huh. They were right. Why *can't* we live in Stowe? We're there all the time anyway. It just clicked. With very little thought, we pivoted. With one week to go, we enrolled our kids in the Stowe school system and put our new, under-construction home up for sale. It felt right. It was a deep inner knowing that the move was right for me, my wife, and our family. We surrendered to the moment. We still took a lot of action in a very short period of time, but we surrendered and Stowe is now home.

LETTING GO OF THE OUTCOME

Surrender is what happens when you let go of the outcome. When you are in the middle of a meeting or negotiating with your kids in the morning, let go of the outcome. It's simple, but not easy. Of course, you want the meeting to go well and you want your kids to be on time for school with a healthy lunch and their completed homework in their backpacks. What we are looking to let go of here is the personal need to get something from those activities going the way we want them to.

We *need* the meeting to go well otherwise we might disappoint someone or we may feel incompetent. We *need* our kids to be model students so that we feel pride, happiness, and maybe a little superior to other parents. What we are unconsciously saying when we work so hard to control the outcomes is, "If it doesn't go exactly how I need it to, then I am not going to be okay inside." Because when the energy isn't what you want or expected, you're disturbed.

Instead, what if you just worked on being okay inside and then anything that happened on the outside—a great meeting or an awesome report card—was just icing on the cake? It doesn't mean that you don't have high standards or expectations. But it does mean that you get focused on the right activities and hold your team, your kids, and your co-workers accountable to those activities. At the same time, you let go of "needing" a certain outcome to feel whole and complete.

Phil Jackson is one of the most prolific coaches in NBA history, coaching his teams to eleven championships. In his book *Eleven Rings: The Soul of Success*, Jackson writes, "The most we can hope for is to create the best possible conditions for success, then let go of the outcome. The ride is a lot more fun that way."

This was often seen as an unpopular opinion. People thought Jackson was throwing in the towel and didn't care about winning or losing. But that couldn't be further from the truth. Jackson knew that his team had put in the work, they had shown up and practiced, they were conditioned and ready to go. They had created the best possible conditions to play the game. And then they let go of the outcome. Whatever was going to happen would happen. Why not just enjoy the experience?

NEED NOTHING AND ENJOY EVERYTHING

In both of the earlier personal examples I shared, there was a deep inner knowing that pointed me in a new direction. I had to trust the feeling, let go of any preferences or expectations (need nothing), and then just lean into enjoying the experience (enjoy everything).

Think about your own moments of surrender. Did you need a certain thing to happen or did you let go of the outcome? What are the things that you truly enjoy in life? What if you could experience that with everything? Let's look at an example.

Every day, Americans drink 400 million cups of coffee. And there are only 332 million Americans (as of 2022). I'm not about to get on a soapbox to talk about the pros and cons of coffee and caffeine consumption. But I think the sheer amount of coffee consumed begs the question: Is coffee a necessity or do people just really like it that much?

Are you a coffee drinker? Do you need it in the morning before you can function? Do you use it to boost your energy in the afternoon? Do you simply love coffee culture and get completely consumed by the latest seasonal blend? Do you unconsciously drink it simply out of a habit you've had since senior year of high school? What positive and/or limiting beliefs do you have around coffee?

We're kind of using coffee here for a stand-in for any of your vices or simple pleasures (depending on how you look at them). We could just as easily switch out coffee for wine, or hot baths, or meditation, or exercise.

Where is the line drawn between doing something because you need the enjoyment and just enjoying the simple pleasures or even the big, splashy events in life? Usually, we indulge in things like a glass of wine or a hot yoga class because we know we're going to get enjoyment out of them—so is that needing or enjoying?

I think needing and enjoying exist on a spectrum and everyone falls a little bit differently on that spectrum with different things. In the early years of my real estate career, I was on the needing end of the coffee spectrum. I was drinking more than I needed to to feel good in my body, but I still thought that I needed a large coffee from Starbucks to start my day. I went through the same evolution with alcohol many years ago. You probably wouldn't even find me on the spectrum of needing alcohol these days; however, if I truly want a glass of pinot noir while sitting next to the fire in the middle of January after skiing all day, I'll have it. And enjoy it. But, I can also take it or leave it. There is no pull there anymore, at least for me. Of course, I am not talking about alcohol addiction here, which often calls for proper treatment.

Occasionally, if I've had a really long week or didn't get a good night's sleep, I may want to reach for a glass of wine or that extra large coffee, respectively. When that happens, I know it's more about needing it than actually enjoying it.

Many of you reading this book have likely used work or building your business as a distraction from facing something more emotionally or spiritually challenging in your life, or as a measure of your worth (and subsequently your success). You *needed* your business to thrive or you *needed* people to depend on you to help complete a work project in order to feel whole and complete. You might have enjoyed your work, but your *need* for it trumped the enjoyment and therefore defeated the point.

There is no right or wrong with coffee, hobbies, work, or any other external thing you have in your life. The key is to be aware of your relationship to those things and let that be your guide in terms of your choices. When you use those pleasures in life to distract you or to ignore reality, it becomes an issue.

If you feel the urge to distract yourself with an external pleasure like Netflix, sleep, meditation, exercise, or answering emails, that's fine. Just know consciously that is what you are doing. Tell yourself you are consciously choosing that coffee because you need to kick up your energy a notch before a big sales call. I've done this before when I feel anxious and I consciously go on a run to release the anxious energy. Coffee and running are tools that are available to us in the external world, so why not use them?

If you are truly enjoying everything, there is no energy behind the coffee, exercise, cars, vacation, relationship, etc. It's great. It's pleasurable. But you don't *need* it to feel whole and complete. You probably have already experienced this feeling before with something in your life—maybe you can take or leave Instagram, or take or leave dogs, or take or leave dessert. You can enjoy it, or not, and you still feel the same. That's great! Start to see that showing up in other areas of your life. Just remember, the moment you need something, you've lost.

What's the Point?

A human being is complete just being human. We are our own destination.
— Matt Haig

Time for a quick check-in. We've let go of preferences and expectations. We don't have any likes or dislikes. We've surrendered to life unfolding. We live in the moment. We need nothing. We enjoy everything. So, what's the point of all this spiritual work, and of our human existence?

WHY ARE YOU HERE?

There are hundreds of billions of stars and trillions of galaxies. We are just a grain of sand in the Sahara Desert. One thousand years from now, there may not even be Americans. What if we all merge into one global culture of Earthians? What if earth isn't even here anymore? If we are so insignificant, what is the point?

Ah, the age-old question of what the heck we're doing on earth as a human. Why are you here? Why am I here?

Here's my answer to that question—for me. Your answer may be a little different than mine, but my answer may help guide you towards your own. I think that the finite (yes, even if it's billions of years from now) nature of the universe, actually makes our brief human experience even more special. So, why am I here? Fundamentally, I know it's to evolve and grow as a spiritual being having a minor physical/human experience. More specifically, my mission for my life is to raise the moment in front of me so that the moment is better off for having passed by me.

I know, I know. The next questions that inevitably follow are, "But then what is all that growth for? What are you evolving for? If one day the earth isn't even going to be here, why does my growth and evolution even matter?" For many, this question can manifest in an even more anxious way, such as "What am I supposed to do with my life!?"

When you die, nothing is going with you—so how can those things have any real meaning? The company you built, your children, the meals you delivered to an assisted living facility, your dogs, your beach house... they will all remain behind. They are part of the physical world and can not follow you into the spiritual world.

When you say the meaning of life is your kids or your financial legacy or the hundreds of people you employed while building a business, it's just not true. That's only another way of saying you want and need the outside thing in order to give you meaning, to make you feel a certain way inside. The external world and material things are the stimulus to get you to feel a certain way inside.

Why not focus on the inside first? Why not work on that? Focus on the inside first and then go out into the world and just play!

PURPOSE & PASSION

The purpose of your life is to live it and work on your inner growth while you're here. Inner growth just means that you are able to let go of the part of you that is preventing you from appreciating the moment in front of you. It's as simple as that. We overcomplicate life so much by putting restrictions and goals and expectations and limits on what our life should be.

In fact, when you stop looking for a plan, purpose, or path to enlightenment or success, then you realize that *you* are the plan. *You* are enlightenment. *You* are the purpose. Not what you do or accomplish—just you. Only you and forever you. The path or purpose is just the mind's way of seeking. Any form of seeking is the mind's way of distracting us from experiencing our true self. When you are no longer seeking, you will find. So, call off your search!

But we live in a 200% world, so inevitably, we're going to be faced with questions of purpose and passion in the external world.

Take this question, for example: "What are you passionate about?" It's a standard interview question that I wish wasn't asked! I understand what people are getting at when they ask the question. They want to know what gets you out of bed every morning, what energizes you, and where you like to spend your time (even if you're not compensated for it). It's a practical and grounded question that begs for a spiritual answer.

What if you were passionate about everything? I mean, why not? If you were filled with joy, inspiration, and enthusiasm whether you were meeting with a client, shopping for groceries, helping your kids research a history paper, or traveling for work, what might life look and feel like?

The point here is that if you need to do something to deal with the world, you might as well bring passion into whatever you are doing. Sure, there is an alignment, a nature, and a personality that everyone has. However, there is no rule that says you can't be passionate for everything you are doing, *and* also change or enhance your outside world at the same time. Be passionate about what you get to do in life—no matter what it is.

Let's say you have an important client meeting and you choose to get on a plane and fly to their office in Colorado, even though you would rather they come to you. You choose to take the meeting and get on the plane. You can now bring your passion, energy, and enthusiasm to the plane ride, or you can complain about why you shouldn't have to fly to Colorado and the client should have come to you. Having passion for everything in life means showing up fully in the moment, no matter what you're doing. If you don't need to do it or life isn't asking you to do it, then don't do it. But if you have said "yes," then make it a "hell yes!" and engage with all you've got.

Don't get me wrong, I understand that there are things we don't like to do. Maybe you don't like your job, but you're choosing to show up every day, anyway. That's a good starting point. Let go of the inner voice that isn't happy with what you're doing and accept that you are choosing right now to go to work instead of calling in sick or quitting. The very fact that you have chosen to show up gives you power—the power to fully engage and be passionate about whatever you're doing. From this place, creativity and contentment can flow, at least in the moment. Yes, continue to look for a new opportunity. But the point is that if you're choosing to do something, do it with the passion that is already within you. What's the alternative? Being pissed about the choice you made? Doesn't sound very fun to me!

There will be moments in life where you will be questioning how you can actually bring passion to the events that are unfolding—attending a memorial service, going through a divorce, or watching your parents' health decline. Perhaps passion is not what you are after in these moments, but you can accept the moment and not push it away or cling to it. The very fact that the moment is happening means it was meant to happen. You can always choose to accept the reality of the situation. Always. From a place of acceptance, you can move forward with more peace, and yes, maybe even a little passion.

Purpose and passion is already within you. Life is too short to do anything else but experience and enjoy it all!

15

Death is Our Greatest Teacher

The day which we fear as our last is but the birthday of eternity.

—Seneca

Speaking of how short life is… a couple of years ago I was getting a haircut downtown like I do every four weeks. My phone rang, I saw it was my dad calling, and I put my phone back down. I call my dad every day, so I knew I would just give him a ring when I was done. Seconds later, he called again. This was not typical behavior, so I asked the stylist to give me a second while I answered the phone. My dad's voice came through loud, panicked, and a little breathless. He told me he thought he was having a heart attack and was driving himself to the hospital. He was understandably shaken, in pain, and scared about what might happen. He kept repeating to himself and me, "I don't want to die. I don't want to die. I don't want to die." And then his mind took over and he began to go through all the worst-case scenarios, should haves, and what ifs.

He was starting to spiral (well, his mind was). So, I cut him off and said, "There is basically one of two things that is going to happen: you are either going to live or you are going to die." Maybe it was the jolt of the harsh truth I shared, but it seemed to refocus and recenter my father. I stayed on the phone with him until he checked himself into the ER and then I joined him there minutes later. My father did end up having quintuple coronary bypass surgery, and he is still strengthening his heart and his faith in the greater universe every day.

Over the course of the twenty-two days that he was in the hospital, we had many long talks about spirituality, the ego, the 200% life, his grandkids, his relationships, his business, and, of course, we talked about death.

One of humans' most common fears is death. At the same time, we understand that it's just a fact of life that we are all going to die someday, so what is there to be afraid of? *The Tibetan Book of Living and Dying* by Sogyal Rinpoche shares this thought: "Perhaps the deepest reason why we are afraid of death is because we do not know who we are."

When a person feels like they have not discovered who they are or what their purpose is, they may be afraid to die because it means that they will no longer have any time to figure it out. This is why I am so adamant that we focus on the inner world first. If you have that deep understanding and peace with yourself, when death comes, you will be unafraid.

This is similar to the concept of optimistic nihilism. Optimistic nihilism is a philosophy that says there is no great meaning of life. Now, contrary to how it sounds, it doesn't mean that life is hopeless and we might as well give up. It's actually the opposite and quite a freeing thought—if we embrace it. If the universe itself is meaningless, then we, in our human form, get to create our own meaning by experiencing ourselves, as well as our internal and external worlds.

Death is an event that happens to everyone, no matter how rich, happy, or successful they are. Don't let your impending death make you give up! Instead, leverage death to help you become more present and to observe your emotions, rather than getting tangled up in them.

After all, it is only your physical body and the ego that dies. The real You, your soul, never dies.

I made peace with death many years ago as part of my spiritual journey. I am not afraid of dying or of death. There is nothing that I have let go unsaid to those I love. I don't have any regrets. I live in the moment and strive to make each moment better for having passed by me. Death taught me that. The knowledge that we only have a very insignificant time here on earth makes life extremely precious. Why waste even one second not truly appreciating the moment you get to experience?

About six months after the surgery, I can say that my father has changed. It took four to five months for him to regain his cognitive ability, and after about six months he started seeing life differently. I think he began to see the fragility of life itself. I think he was an individual who always knew intellectually that he would die, but when faced with his own mortality, he realized, "Shit, I really am going to die."

My dad has started to take things slower, to do more things that bring him joy even if that means less money. That was a big lesson we worked through. Having a super high-quality life doesn't mean you need to make a certain amount of money. It means truly appreciating the simple things and the moments you have... a trail walk, coffee in the morning while watching the sunrise, sitting in a deer blind, building a bench out of a fallen tree.

In fact, this "simple" version of life is not only more fulfilling for him and anyone else who really stops and evaluates their own life, but it also equates to financial freedom almost instantly. Instead of hustling harder to hit a certain income or net worth, what if you added to your life by subtracting and simplifying? You can get to freedom in the external world so much faster!

Freedom in the financial or external world aside, what's really happening here is that you are finding an internal sense of peace, and that is absolute freedom. But before we can get there, we still need to peel back a few layers of the 100% external world.

WHAT DO PEOPLE REALLY WANT?

What do people really want in life? What do you want? This is a fundamental question for humans. We ask it of ourselves, we ask it of our spouses, and we ask our employees and team members too.

WHAT DO YOU WANT?

Another way to think of it is, what are you after? On the surface, we would get thousands of different answers about what people want, such as a cat, to learn to ski, an affordable apartment in NYC, a Rivian R1S, to swim in the ocean, to hire three new employees, to have two kids, to go apple picking with family, to net $1 million dollars a year, to become a yoga teacher, to skydive, to get married, to run a marathon, to heal their adrenal fatigue, to travel to Paris, and on, and on.

However, if we drill down on each of these answers, what we find is that everyone is actually after the same thing: the juice of life, the shakti, the spirit, the flow of energy that lights you up from the inside out and creates endless amounts of joy, love, creativity, and enthusiasm. You want to know yourself. You want to experience yourself. You want to bring all that unconditional love, joy, creativity, and enthusiasm into the physical world. You want the feeling of pure and blissful consciousness here on earth.

People think that what they really want is a car or vacation or a relationship or a house or to own their own business. And that very well may be true. But that's only part of the story. There is nothing stopping you from going after those things, but if you are going after those things in the material/physical world in order to get the inner fulfillment, then you're not exactly doing it wrong, you're just doing it indirectly.

It's not really your fault, either! We've been conditioned through our culture and society that if we get what we want, we'll feel great! At least for a little while. Our egoic state of consciousness eats up these little successes and stores them away and says, "More, more!" Just the fact of setting a goal, working towards it, and imagining how you will feel when you get it can make you happy and will feed the ego just enough to keep you going back for more. The egoic state of consciousness is always seeking. Seeking more experiences, more money, more vacations, more successes, more hits of happiness to keep it going. Unfortunately, it's a trap. You end up on a hamster wheel of seeking, gaining, getting "happy hits," and then once that hit of happiness is gone, you're back in the cycle of seeking and gaining more and more over and over again.

The mind will keep telling you that if only you could earn $50,000 more, you'll be happy, or if you can finally buy a new house with a pool, you'll be happy. But the mind lies! Sure, go get those things and tell me how long it is before your mind and your egoic state of consciousness are looking for the next thing to make you feel happy and okay inside.

Particularly in business, we find ourselves constantly searching for that next thing. We hit one milestone or income goal and it's onto the next—looking for more power, money, fame, pleasure, significance, energy and happiness. But to what end? And *when* does it end? Well, if you are only playing in the 100% of the external world, then you will be searching your entire life.

What people really want is the other 100% of life, the inner world that produces the juice and energy of life. This is where You live. There is You and then there is everything else. Focus on the You—the inner world—first, and everything else will unfold exactly as it should.

16

Learn, Work, and Play Every Day

For everything there is a season, a time for every activity under heaven. A time to be born and a time to die. A time to plant and a time to harvest. A time to kill and a time to heal. A time to tear down and a time to build up. A time to cry and a time to laugh. A time to grieve and a time to dance. A time to scatter stones and a time to gather stones. A time to embrace and a time to turn away. A time to search and a time to quit searching. A time to keep and a time to throw away. A time to tear and a time to mend. A time to be quiet and a time to speak. A time to love and a time to hate. A time for war and a time for peace.
Ecclesiastes 3:1-8 NLT

While our purpose in life is to work on our inner growth, there is a whole other 100% external world that is there for us to engage with, enjoy, and experience. There is a season, a time, for every activity and experience in the inner and outer world.

Society has taught us to live a very linear life. We're born, we go to school for over a decade, then many will continue and go to college or grad school, then you get a dog, get married, land your dream job, buy a house, have a kid or two, refinance your home, get a promotion, remodel your kitchen, buy a bigger house, retire, travel the world for the next two years, and then come home and help raise the grand-kids.

We spend the first twenty or so years of our life in this neat little box of learning. We spend the next forty years in a working box, and then if we're lucky, we get twenty to thirty years left to unwrap the box of playing.

When I was in my early twenties, I realized that the linear life was not for me. I didn't want to work for the next forty years and never play. And I didn't want all of my learning to be behind me. I was not looking for the holy grail of work-life balance. I was looking for work-life integration, work-life harmony, work-life presence. I wanted to learn, work, and play every day as part of my 200% life. You can too.

Here's what that looks like in practice for me:

- Daily exercise. Learning, working, and playing depending on how new or challenging the workout is.
- Reading. Usually learning by listening to Audible during a workout or while commuting to the office.
- Working. This is both work, play, and learning for me. Business is also a sport. For example, I'm always learning how to be a better leader. I've created a "job" for myself where I can insert myself into the business when and where I want. This works for any career. You won't love everything you do all the time, but if you can bring the joy inside of you to whatever you are doing, then your work will also become your play.
- Attending swim meets for kids. I learn how to be a better father, listener and practice my patience during kids' events.
- Bike rides with the family. Full-on play! Well, most of the

time…

- Making dinner. This can be work and learning too. If I'm making a new meal or really focusing on my nutrition and macros, then I'm learning and working.

Those are just a few examples for you. My goal is to make sure I incorporate learning, working, and playing into my day every day. It doesn't have to be hours and hours of work, nor does it need to be hours and hours of play or learning. Some days will be mostly learning, with a little play and work thrown in, and some days will be all work, but I am purposeful about making sure I get play and learning in there too.

When it comes to choosing how to allocate my time across learning, working, and playing, I like to think about this question, particularly when it comes to work: "How good, how productive, how impactful can I be in the amount of time I'm willing to work?" If I'm only willing to work thirty hours a week, then how do I need to show up and where do I need to focus my time within those thirty hours to make the biggest contribution to the company and my team?

It's never about the number of hours; it's always about the intention and energy that you bring to the moment. As we discussed in Chapter 14, we can bring passion and joy to everything that we do. And we don't have to wait until we retire to truly live. Let's be honest, it's probably going to be more fun to play while you're thirty-seven, than seventy-three. Or is it?

IMPROVING YOUR HEALTH SPAN

As we discuss the importance of cultivating and growing the inner world, let us not forget that we are living a human experience and we have a body to take care of. Jim Rohn, American entrepreneur, author and motivational speaker, said, "Take care of your body. It's the only place you have to live." And I might add that it's the only place that we have to live while we're here on earth. Why wouldn't we want to take care of our physical body in order to allow us a longer health span (the period of life spent in good health, free from the chronic diseases and disabilities of aging) in which to work on our inner growth?

I'm not going to tell you what to eat, how to exercise, how long to sleep, what your target heart rate should be, or that you should give up alcohol and coffee, because everybody is different. But I do want you to know that once you start to do real personal and spiritual growth, what you should eat and drink, and how you should support your body for health and longevity starts to become very clear. You start to become more aligned with nature and *your* nature. A hawk doesn't wake up and think about eating grass, any more than a deer would think about eating a rabbit. Humans struggle with how to approach their health and wellness because of the interference of the mind. Let that go and listen to the inner voice. It will guide you towards the most natural and supportive way to take care of your body.

Now, I know I told you that I'm not going to tell you what to do. Don't worry, I'm not! But I do want to point out a few wellness areas that you might want to explore and optimize to best support your health span. Remember, it's a 200% life! We have to nurture our physical self, just as much as our spiritual self. They go hand in hand.

1. SLEEP
    Quality sleep is so underrated, especially for hard-charging entrepreneurs and busy professionals. You should target seven to nine hours of sleep each night. To get that quality sleep in, have a consistent bedtime and bedtime routine (no screens at least thirty minutes before bed!). Avoid alcohol. Keep your room cool and dark. And during the day, make sure to exercise and get some natural sunlight. Waking up at the same time every morning is helpful too.

If you want to take your sleep to the next level, you may want to invest in some sleep accessories such as a weighted blanket, a cooling system like EightSleep, earthing sheets, a sunrise alarm clock, room darkening curtains or a sleep mask, a white noise machine, and a high quality mattress and pillow.

Why is good sleep so important? It improves concentration, can reduce the risk of heart disease and stroke, decreases inflammation and depression, improves your immune system, positively affects emotions and social interactions, and boosts your brain health.

2. STRESS MANAGEMENT
Stress, particularly chronic stress, can have significant negative effects on the body, including high blood pressure, heart disease, obesity, diabetes, depression and anxiety, gastrointestinal issues, stroke, sleep issues, memory and concentration impairment, and heart attack. Suffice it to say, focusing on stress management is key to improving your life span.

Stress management can look a little different for everyone; however, some common stress management practices include exercise, meditation, yoga, journaling, therapy, positive social connection, being in nature, participating in one of your favorite hobbies, and breathing exercises. It's important to find a stress management and stress reduction practice that works for you—*consistently*. You don't want to wait to work on your stress reduction when you're on the brink of a crisis. By having a consistent practice, when stress arises (and it will), you will be able to get your mind, body, and soul back to a neutral state more quickly.

3. HYDRATION

Our bodies are made up of about 60% water. We're a living organism! Therefore we must water ourselves every day. A good rule of thumb is to drink half your body weight in ounces per day (but always check with a health professional!). If you weigh 185 pounds, drinking about ninety-three ounces of water a day would help keep you hydrated.

Staying hydrated helps regulate your body temperature, keeps your joints lubricated, prevents infection, delivers nutrients to your cells, keeps your organs functioning properly, improves brain performance, increases your energy, assists with weight management, improves detoxification, and keeps your heart healthier.

4. MOVEMENT

There are thousands of workout programs, training apps, and fitness classes available to us with just a touch of a button on our phones. Take advantage of them if that's something you're into. But movement doesn't have to be complicated. Walk, go for a hike, stretch, swim, do some yoga in your living room, head to the playground with your kids, or go skiing. Personally, I love a three to five minute foam roll a few times a day too.

Just like sleep, stress management, hydration, and nutrition, the key here is consistency. Our bodies were made to move. So get up and get moving, whatever that looks like to you.

5. SUPPORTIVE NUTRITION

Nutrition is an area where you really want to get to know yourself and your body. Some bodies thrive on meat and fruit, others do best with a plant-based diet, and still others run optimally on bread and cheese.

What I want you to think about here is finding the best foods to fuel your body to support your level of activity and lifestyle. And, you can never go wrong by focusing on whole foods (non-processed).

I would also be remiss if I didn't mention alcohol consumption. I like a full-bodied glass of pinot noir just as much as the next person, but extreme moderation here is key. There is no nutritional value to alcohol (the positive effects of resveratrol in red wine is a myth). All alcohol consumption—even a few drinks a week—can have negative impacts on our bodies, our liver, cognitive ability, and more. Studies have shown that only one to two drinks *per month* have no negative effects. Again, we are not referring to alcohol addiction here, wherein any amount of alcohol would be detrimental. I'll get off my soapbox now, but just consider your alcohol consumption as you think about supportive nutrition and your health span.

As you are determining your daily schedule, remember to set aside time to work, learn, and play every day and play full-out in this 200% life!

Please note: Always check with your doctor before embarking on a new diet or exercise routine.

17

Your Identity

The privilege of a lifetime is to become who you really are.

—Carl Jung

When we learn, work, and play in this 200% life, it's important to take a look at the roles we are playing in the external world.

In Chapter 4, we talked about who we really are inside and that we are not our mind, our thoughts, our body, or our emotions. Who we are in the 100% internal world is a spiritual being. However, there is the 100% external, physical world where the roles we play and the identities we embody serve a practical purpose. But they can also cause confusion and suffering if we don't understand the nuances around identity and how to use them, rather than allow them to use us.

For many of us, the answer to the question, "Who are you?" will be some variation of "I'm a CEO" or "I'm a mother," or father, dentist, sister, husband, accountant, or some other role. Of course, we all know that those words or identities don't really get to the core of who we are, but think back again on your gut-answer to that question. How attached are you to the role that first came into your mind? What would happen if tomorrow you became an empty-nester, or you lost your job? Identifying too strongly with any one role may lead to suffering when that role suddenly vanishes, and the attachment to an identity can limit your thinking and growth in the first place.

Identity is a funny thing. When I'm introducing myself at a conference, I'm Adam Hergenrother, CEO & Entrepreneur. When I'm meeting people at a family gathering with my in-laws, I'm Adam, Sarah's husband. When I'm on a ski trip, I'm Asher's dad. Your identity—how you (and others) label and categorize yourself within your world—is a powerful thing. But it can either be empowering or crippling depending on how much external validation you attach to it. Did I change between the conference and the family party? Nope. But how I labeled myself for the benefit of society did.

Do not confuse your identity with who you are at the core. Identity is an external manifestation of how you, and others, see you and how you believe you fit into society. Your identity (or identities) are simply constructs of the mind. These various identities are just roles you play in the world. They serve a purpose. When you're at the office, you may need to take off your elementary school dance chaperone hat and put on your CEO hat. When you leave work, you may need to take off your CEO hat and put on your patient and attentive partner hat. You can be a chameleon, shifting your identity based on the audience or who you need to present yourself as in any given situation. Being able to separate your role from who you really are is essential to being a better leader and living a more fulfilling life, both in your personal and professional world.

In *Love in the Time of Cholera*, author Gabriel Garcia Marquez writes, "He allowed himself to be swayed by his conviction that human beings are not born once and for all on the day their mothers give birth to them, but that life obliges them over and over again to give birth to themselves." Part of our human nature is to grow, evolve, take on new roles, and be "born again" many times throughout our lives. Being aware of what is happening is the key.

Over the course of your lifetime, you may fiercely protect an identity that you believe represents who you really are inside. More commonly, though, our egos have created such inflexible identities that we become afraid to let them go. After all, they may have protected us in the past or served a purpose to help us achieve whatever external or material success we've achieved. Why would we want to let those identities go?

Because they aren't really you. It's just the ego putting up a really good front. Maybe you know that your internal life (your truth) is not matching what you are living and projecting on the outside. Are you willing to share your truth with the world or is your fear holding you back?

Maybe you are still working on surrendering and peeling back your ego layer by layer. Just remember, your identity is not you. There can be a ton of internal conflict around identity. Identity crises are real!

Let me give you an example. Ava is a successful lawyer who kicks ass and takes names daily. She works 80+ hours a week, gets up at 5 a.m. to email clients, and works well into the night on depositions or case reviews. She has received several Rising Star awards, has started a blog to document her trials and triumphs as a young attorney in a small coastal town, and she takes a minimum of one pro bono case per month. She is Ava the Attorney morning, noon, and night. From the outside, she has it all: a successful career, recognition in her industry, a promotion on the horizon, a supportive partner at home, and a new puppy.

But what we don't see is that Ava works every weekend, eats takeout at her desk, falls into bed at midnight, and mindlessly watches old episodes of *Friends*. She hasn't had a real date with her husband in months, she doesn't exercise, and she often cancels plans with friends because she can't fathom one more commitment on her calendar. Before becoming Ava the Attorney, Ava was multidimensional, loved spending time outside, could get lost in a good book for hours, and had an Etsy shop where she sold her artwork. But she has lost herself along the way to becoming Ava the Attorney. That is her only identity, which she wears proudly, but she also often feels like a fraud. She has more to offer the world, and while that identity has served her well over the past ten years, she wants more and knows she is more than just an attorney. Full on identity crisis. Ava's soul is crying out, not for more, per se, but for the truth. Authenticity. For a fuller, more well-rounded life that feels true to who Ava is and fuels her soul. Does Ava have to give up her identity and success as an attorney to also be spiritually fulfilled?

On the inside, Ava's true being is waiting to be uncovered, but she has only allowed one part of herself to shine through: Ava the Attorney. The world sees her in one way, and one way only, and Ava is constantly trying to live up to that expectation while sacrificing other parts of who she is.

But let me tell you something. You, or Ava, are not doing yourself or the world any favors by stifling those other parts of who you really are!

It will not be easy, but it will change your world if you are able to align your external identity with what's going on inside. That's what living an authentic life looks like.

Ava may continue to hide behind her attorney identity for many years until it becomes so suffocating that she breaks and is forced to make a change. But it doesn't have to get to that point. You can crawl your way out of the deep hole of identity that you have placed yourself in or that someone else has labeled you as.

The strongest desire in humans is the desire to stay consistent with who we think we are (i.e. the identity we have created). Every choice we make, every action we take, is based on the desire to stay comfortable, to stay consistent, with who we believe we are. From the clothes we wear, to the partners we attract, to the jobs we take, to the sports we play, to the people we hang out with... all of those choices are based on an effort to stay consistent with who we think we are.

But remember, identities only work for the short term. They can certainly serve a purpose, but they should not hold you hostage. We are not the roles we play. We are behind that label, that identity, that role, or that job, witnessing the world. You can either hide behind an identity that you or someone else has created, or you can work to find out who you really are on the inside.

When it comes to the roles and identities we play, it's never about how many hours we work or contribute to our identity. The problem is that we are attached to our identity in the first place. For example, you might be working thirty hours a week at a gig you've had for a while, until you get the opportunity to start a new division at a large company. Now you're working sixty-five hours a week and enjoying every part of what you are creating and you're bringing your inner enthusiasm and applying it to work (which doesn't even really feel like work to you!).

Conversely, you may have been running a company as an operations professional for a decade, but then realize that your true joy comes from leading, coaching, and teaching. You take this authentic passion and bring it to coaching your kid's baseball team, volunteering on a local board, and eventually take a position that doesn't require travel or sixty-five hour work-weeks. You make less money, but you are so much more fulfilled.

In either case, you become detached from your identity as a corporate professional or freelancer and are flowing into a new phase of life. Not just *a* phase of life, but the phase of life where you are in true alignment.

As I mentioned before, roles can be helpful in the external world. It's important to understand and acknowledge the various roles we have, and be able to switch into a certain role depending on what the present moment calls for. All the while knowing that your true starting position is one of deep authenticity and alignment with the inner you.

What it really comes down to as a conscious person is knowing when to step into a particular role, but not becoming attached to the role. You can move into an identity or role when life asks you to do so, while knowing that this is not really you. Think about the roles you play in your family. Sometimes you need to be the disciplinarian with your kids, and sometimes it's okay for you to show up as their friend.

Steve Jobs is a great example of someone who lived a life that was true to himself, eccentricities and all. Jobs practiced Zen and had a relentless drive towards simplicity in everything that he did. He brought these parts of himself to his role as CEO of Apple. He was a simplicity maven who just happened to bring that into the tech world. When he was forced out of his own company, Jobs founded NeXT. New role, CEO of NeXT, same relentlessly driven, infamously direct style, and a continued obsession with simplicity.

At some point, you will be faced with the choice to let go of the identities that your ego has created. This is where the deep work that you've been doing will come into play. One of the most important characteristics of a conscious human is to be willing to be untethered from any of the roles they play. They know the roles are tools that they can use, but they are more than the roles. Once that awareness has been established, it will provide more clarity than anything that your ego or mind could generate. From this space, you will have complete freedom to interact with whatever role you need to serve or contribute to the moment in front of you.

Congratulations. When you detach yourself from your identities and roles, you've peeled back one more layer of your spiritual journey.

18

The MVVBP of the External World

The happiest people discover their own nature and match their life to it.

—Ray Dalio

When you really begin to see the truth—that there is another 100% of life available to us on the inside—you may start questioning the external world all together. In the past, you've made decisions based on how they would make you feel—happy, devastated, excited, sad, energized, significant, etc. You were either trying to get a feeling or push away a feeling. But, the further you go down the spiritual path, you realize that nothing in the external world can truly make you feel one way or another (at least deeply or sustainably).

The next questions that inevitably arise are: Why does it matter what decision I make, then? If I'm okay with everything, then nothing really matters, right? Does it even matter if I make a good or bad decision?

Yes, it does matter! Remember, we are living a 200% life. There are going to be times when we have to put on a certain identity (father, CEO, brother, lacrosse coach, husband) and make decisions from one of those roles that we play in the external world. You play the role that you need to play at any given moment. But those aren't who You are. External world decisions are more surface-level decisions.

For us entrepreneurs, business is just a game that we have been pulled to play. For others, it's parenting, volunteering, teaching, content creation, or intraprenuership. We all have our own unique nature. The deeper decisions are when we are making decisions about who we are and how we want to feel inside (without needing external stimuli). And then when you do go back into the external world to play, when you're speaking in front of employees or going mountain biking with your friends, you are making micro-decisions every second, spontaneously and effortlessly.

Ultimately, useful and skilled decision making is all about clarity. It's knowing when you need to put on your external hat and interact with the world, without letting it affect who you are inside. For example, let's say you are going through a divorce and you receive an aggressive and accusatory email from your soon-to-be ex-wife. You immediately feel angry, and resentful energy rises up in your body. You click "reply" and start typing away—IN ALL CAPS. You know it will make you feel better to discharge your feelings in that email, but how helpful will that really be? Pause. 3, 2, 1… Relax. Get centered and back to a neutral state. You're fine. Delete the email you were writing.

A more helpful decision and action is to respond to the email cordially and succinctly without attachment. You don't need to be right. You just need to move forward with clarity. Interacting with each moment from this place is a gift to those around you but, honestly, it's even more of a gift to yourself. Why get riled up about something when you can completely control how you feel and engage with others and the world from that place? Who wouldn't want to do that? It feels so much better!

This is a great place to operate from. Keep practicing letting go. The next step in your spiritual evolution is to not write the email at all, and just respond from that neutral and centered place. That is emotional and spiritual maturity.

When you have this maturity and clarity, things begin to unfold in new ways. Decisions drive the trajectory of our life. So, why wouldn't we want to be as clear as possible in order to make the best decisions that align with our true nature? I mean, we're going to play in the external world, so we might as well make high quality and supportive decisions while we're at it!

Several years ago, I was pulled towards a new challenge of competing in Ironman races. That initial decision kicked off a series of micro-decisions that needed to be made to support that larger goal. Training for an Ironman is very time intensive. I needed at least one full training day a week and I knew the weekends wouldn't work (weekends are family time!). So, I needed to allocate my Fridays to training. This led me to clearing my entire work calendar one day a week and then maximizing and arranging my schedule Monday through Thursday to ensure I focused on the most important things for the business during the time I had allocated to work.

Turns out, for the most part, I didn't even need that Friday for work. For the next three years, our businesses continued to grow and thrive. I competed in twenty half or full Ironmans in three and a half years and even qualified for the 70.3 World Championship race in South Africa. The point? When you are clear on what is most important to you in life and business, you can make the conscious decision to create a schedule (and ultimately a life) that supports those activities.

When you have clarity, you have a deeper understanding of what you're supposed to do. Life will never fail you with this. Life is a dance, but remember, life is always in the lead. If you embrace this idea and continue to let go, you will always be moving in the direction life wants you to go. Now, it may not be where *you* think you should go (which is what your mind and ego will try to tell you). But this is where a little faith and trust comes into play. If you are committed to this spiritual journey and doing the work, a lot of life's decisions will become much clearer.

Yes, you will still need to make decisions. Just make each decision as close as you can to where life is leading you. You won't get it perfect, but if you follow this path of right action, you can't go wrong. Each choice will lead you to further growth.

YOUR MVVBP (MISSION, VISION, VALUES, BELIEFS, PERSPECTIVE)

One tool that can be particularly useful in the external world is an MVVBP (Mission, Vision, Values, Beliefs, Perspective). It can operate as a framework and roadmap to help you keep the deeper understanding and meaning of your life front and center.

In *Principles: Life and Work*, founder of Bridgewater Associates Ray Dalio writes, "Principles are fundamental truths that serve as the foundations for behavior that gets you what you want out of life. They can be applied again and again in similar situations to help you achieve your goals." Much like principles, an MVVBP can be a great exercise for clarity, especially when you let go of expectations or the need for a certain outcome. Don't think about what sounds good or what other people want for you.

Before you write down your MVVBP, sit in silence for ten to thirty minutes, meditate, or go for a walk outside, and then sit down and write without editing yourself and see what shows up.

Here is my MVVBP as an example.

Mission: Why Am I Alive? What Is My Mission Here?

I am a spiritual being that grows daily. I am aligned and interacting with the moment that is in front of me so that the moment is better off for having passed by my consciousness. I am operating from a place of being first, doing second. Everything I do is an expression of who I am. I have asked the deepest questions in life and un-covered the deepest answers. I am a spiritual and business teacher bridging the two. I am a conscious being full of energy. I help my family and kids learn who they are, why they are here, and how to be first, and then use unconditional love, joy and enthusiasm to create a physical experience.

Vision: Where Am I Going?

(Note: Write this part in the present tense, as if you have already created this vision.)

I've built a business that fosters personal, spiritual, and professional growth first. People, our leadership team, and relationships are the foundational success of my life and our company's existence. Wealth is abundant at every level inside our organization. We are a conscious company that plays full out, laughs, exudes joy, and loves every struggle as much as every success.

Values: What Is Important To Me?

Spiritual development at the highest level. Financial freedom. Spiritual freedom. Physical freedom. Social freedom. Living a life of unconditional love and joy that is demonstrated in each moment that passes by me.

Beliefs: What Do I Believe To Be True?

We are all spiritual beings having a minor physical experience. Therefore, there is no judgment on how someone lives this out. Each one of us has an agenda for our soul that awakens the larger body of consciousness. If we operate from a place of being first, then the doing part of being human is nothing but fun, watching ourselves experience ourselves.

Perspective: How Do You View Yourself And Your Situation At Any Given Moment?

I am grateful for being alive. I am grateful for smiling and bringing joy into each moment. I am grateful for being a conscious leader and teacher throughout this physical world. I am grateful for having fulfillment first, then acting, creating, and building each day. I enjoy each breath. I love and lead myself first.

Keep your MVVBP somewhere you can see and reference it frequently. As you are faced with challenges and decisions in life and business, use your MVVBP as your guiding principles and North Star. As you progress in your spiritual and personal growth, you will likely become so tuned in to your inner knowing that you may not need to read your MVVBP anymore. However, it is also a valuable tool to use with your employees, co-workers, family, and friends. You know what your values, truth, and North Star are. Share it with those closest to you so that they, too, can understand a bit more about who you are and where you are going. They may just decide to join you!

19

Consciousness at Work

We are all connected and therefore should seek understanding with each other.

—Vishen Lakhiani

All of the information that you've learned in this book so far, plus the inner work you are doing, can be brought to your company, employees, and team members. In fact, one of the special parts of working on your inner world is sharing your experiences with others and inviting them along for the ride. As an entrepreneur, business owner, leader, or employee, I think we have a duty to bring consciousness to work in any way that we can.

WHAT DOES CONSCIOUSNESS AT WORK LOOK LIKE?

Most people use their work as a way to bolster their ego and escape from themselves. They hide behind a title, they ignore their feelings and fears by taking on too many projects, or they micromanage others because they feel out of control in their own lives. Work becomes a place where people go to distract themselves from themselves! They are not okay inside, so they use work to strengthen their egos and personal mind by gaining power, prestige, and praise.

But there is a different way to approach work and life! Consciousness at work (and in life) means letting go of—and getting out of—the personal mind so that you are no longer using work as a way to feel good inside. Instead, flip the script! You can use work to liberate yourself instead of distracting and trapping yourself. That is why I always go back to one of my core principles, "Business is nothing but a conduit for personal growth." What better way is there to work on yourself than through the various challenges and issues that arise when dealing with clients, employees, managers, investors, owners, and customers every day?

WORK ON YOURSELF AT WORK

Throughout your time as a business owner or employee, there will inevitably be cycles of dissatisfaction. You're working long hours and not getting paid what you think you deserve. You're having trouble finding talented individuals to join your team. You're feeling unchallenged and uninspired. You're not exactly sure what it is, but you are dissatisfied with your job.

But is it really the job, or is it you? If you were filled with love, joy, and enthusiasm, you could be doing the same job and not be dissatisfied. So it's not the job in and of itself that causes dissatisfaction. It's likely another disturbance arising that needs to be released.

Now, this doesn't mean you have to stay at the company or at the same job forever. It simply means that if you can allow the disturbance to work its way through you, you can then return to a neutral state and act with clarity. As you let the event unfold, you let go of the part that is limiting you, and the world starts to move in ways to support you without you having to force anything or "make" anything happen. You'll start to get raises, new and interesting projects will come your way, you may change positions in your company, or get a promotion. True inspiration at work comes from within you—you are already inspiration itself. When you approach work from this place, you begin to raise the energy and vibrational frequency of everyone around you, creating business and career growth for you and others.

My starting position is that I use my work to work on myself everyday.

Let's take meetings as an example. Meetings can be emotionally charged for a variety of reasons—people trying to prove themselves, egos, conflicting opinions and ideas. As a leader (no matter what your job title is), it's up to you to be clear and centered each time you enter a room, in person or virtually, in order to have the radical conversations we need in today's business world to effect positive change. "Radical conversations" means you are clear, vulnerable, neutral, concise, and open-minded. The only way you can have radical conversations is if you go into them not needing to be right. When we don't have personal energy behind a decision, we see things more clearly and make better decisions.

Check yourself at the door. What is your intention going into this meeting? Is there a personal part of you that is trying to prove something to yourself or others? Are you going into the meeting to be right or are you going into the meeting to contribute? The most effective meetings are those where there are no egos present or running the meeting, where ideas are exchanged, and a solution or decision is made based on the best interests of the organization, not the best decision to appease someone's ego.

True inspiration at work comes from within. When you approach all of your work from that place, the rest (raise, promotion, profit, success, satisfaction, etc.) will come.

HOW DOES THE EGO SHOW UP AT WORK?

The ego really likes to show up at work. You may recognize some of the following examples since I'm sure you've experienced one or two of them over the course of your career thus far.

Your ego shows up at work by needing to be right or needing to "win" at having your idea implemented, a project assignment, or during a simple conversation. When you enter into dialogue with colleagues needing the conversation to go your way, that's your ego leading the conversation, not you. A lot of leaders hide behind bravado and this need to have all the answers, but in the end they are poorly served by their ego. It holds them back from being a curious and conscious leader. It can hold them back from reaching higher levels of success, gaining respect from their co-workers, and it even can hinder them from attracting and retaining employees.

A more conscious approach would be to cultivate curiosity and vulnerability. When entering conversations, you must let go of your need to be right and, instead, go into the conversation wanting to find the best answer or solution for the team or the company. Listen. Ask questions. Stay open minded. And leave your ego at the door.

Another way the ego shows up at work is when employees or leaders take on too many projects, withhold information, or refuse to delegate work. This is usually due to their fear of no longer being able to contribute, wanting to be the smartest person in the room (or at least the one with all the information), or having a bit of martyr syndrome. This is all ego at work. Your ego wants to be seen as valuable, so it ends up engaging in counterproductive behaviors.

A more conscious approach would be to make peace with delegating and become a master at helping team members be their best. After all, you can only do so much as an individual contributor. When you learn to lead others by letting go, you can maximize your reach and impact throughout the company. What's more valuable than that?

One other common way the ego infiltrates our work lives is via imposter syndrome. Imposter syndrome is when one feels a persistent inadequacy despite evidence of success. This often happens when new team members are hired (and you feel competition or jealousy emerge) or when an individual gets a promotion. Imposter syndrome can even happen when things are going well for you, like you are invited to speak at an industry conference or asked to lead a new division. Regardless of the situation, the ego rears its ugly head and has you questioning your worth. This can lead to poor decision making, unprofessional or uncongenial behavior, and even self-sabotage.

A more conscious approach would be to first acknowledge that your ego is taking over and create some separation between you and it. Recognize that as your leadership grows or new employees are hired, your role will shift. Often, leaders end up "doing" less and their work becomes more about reading, thinking, planning, and strategizing. It can feel like they are making less of a contribution, but that's just not true. Their contribution and work simply looks different.

There are many ways the ego can show up at work. Be aware that this can happen and work to quickly identify it when it does. Remember, you are not your ego, your mind, or your identity. Move behind it all. From that place of clarity, you will be able to do your best work.

CONSCIOUS COMMUNICATION AT WORK

Several years ago, an employee came to me with the question, "How come I didn't get that promotion?" And, man, it immediately triggered my ego! The more I thought about it, the more fired up I became. Now, I've done enough personal growth work to know that when my mind and emotions start reeling, it's an indicator that I have inner work to do. I know that if I'm getting triggered, it's my soul's way of telling me "Go deeper. There's more to learn here."

I immediately knew that I could not have a conversation in that state and asked if I could take some time to think about it and get back to this individual in a few days. It happened to be a Friday, so that gave me the weekend to really reflect on the situation and do the work I needed to do in order to get a handle on my thoughts and emotions and regain clarity.

Ultimately, I learned a lot from this experience that can be applied to all sorts of difficult conversations with employees. The goal is gaining extreme clarity so you can lead others through the experience. As Brené Brown, author of *Dare to Lead*, says, "Clarity is kind." Often difficult conversations at work are a minefield of emotions for everyone involved, but as the leader, it's your job to step up and guide the others through that minefield so that you all make it to the other side safely, and you become a stronger team as a result.

If you're a leader, you will inevitably have difficult conversations with employees. There's no escaping it. Here are the steps you can take to make sure you're consciously leading your employees through challenging conversations and to a positive solution.

1. LISTEN

    When an issue is brought to your attention or you bring a challenge to your co-worker or employee, make sure you listen more than you speak. You likely already have your assumptions and arguments at the ready, but they will do no good for anyone if you don't fully understand the issue at hand, and ask the other person's feelings and thoughts about it. Start there. Seek to understand. Ask questions. And make sure there is an agreement about the issue at hand before going any further.

2. SET BOUNDARIES

As I mentioned, I knew I could not have that conversation with my employee right then and there. Do not—I repeat—do not ever enter into a difficult conversation with an employee before you've had time to reflect on it and you feel entirely clear about the situation. And I use "clear" not only to mean mental clarity, but emotional clarity as well. Make sure you are unemotionally attached so you can think of the situation and not feel emotionally triggered by it. If you're feeling your emotions or thoughts rise up and snowball in many directions, you are not clear. So first set the boundary so that you can clean your inner house.

And if it's a situation that needs to be addressed immediately (because some conversations just can't wait), use "3, 2, 1… Relax," another breathing technique or do a quick twenty-minute meditation to center yourself. Once you're centered, then have your meeting.

3. REMEMBER THAT IT'S NOT PERSONAL

In this particular situation, my employee had been with me for many years and we've been through a lot together. At first it was really challenging for me not to take the question personally. My ego wanted to spin that story into a nasty web of "who done it?" Or really, "who is wrong?" And with my ego running the show, obviously the answer wasn't me! But I've learned through personal development work and meditation that ultimately no experience is personal. There are an infinite number of things that must happen for any moment to come into fruition and be exactly as it is. Even though our egos may want to make a situation all about us, the wiser part of us knows that no moment is truly personal.

4. LET GO OF THE PART OF YOU THAT WANTS TO BE RIGHT

Let's be honest… no matter how much inner work we've done, it can still be very hard to let go of the part of us that wants to be right. So this step is very important, and I use the technique "3-2-1… Relax" to let go of the part of me that is insisting on being right. I count down from three and then relax behind the emotions. I often even silently say to myself "let go…" and use my breath to release the tension. Sometimes I may have to repeat this five, ten or twenty times, but ultimately, I'm able to let go of the need to be right if I'm truly committed to that goal. And as a leader, you have to be committed.

Look, if someone is bringing you a conflicting piece of information and you might be wrong, then great, you just saved your company from potential risks. Or maybe you are right and your team members just validated your decision by asking questions and challenging your thinking. Ultimately, do you really want to be right, or do you want what is best for the company?

5. PUT YOURSELF IN THE OTHER PERSON'S SHOES

The old saying "Don't judge someone until you've walked a mile in their shoes" is really important here. The irony is that once you've walked a mile in someone else's shoes, it's pretty much impossible to judge. When I took this step, that's when I got the extreme clarity I was looking for. As I viewed the situation through this employee's eyes, the phrase "job vs. leadership" came to me, and I knew exactly how I needed to respond. In short, because I viewed the situation from his perspective, I was able to see the blind spot that led him to ask why he didn't get the promotion in the first place. He is doing an amazing job at his *job*. He is a total 10/10 when it comes to his day-to-day tasks. But what he wasn't taking into account was his leadership skills. The conversation we needed to have was about how he's closer to a 4/10 when it comes to leadership. That was something concrete that we could discuss and I could help with. With that, I not only found clarity, but compassion and a path forward that would help this individual grow.

6. GET CLEAR ON A SOLUTION AND THEN
    LET GO OF THE OUTCOME
    Once we had found clarity about the issue at hand, we were able to come up with a solution and plan of action. The employee and I decided to work more intentionally on his leadership skills and growth. I chose several books and podcasts for him to read and listen to that we would discuss over the next several months.

    He walked away from the conversation understanding my position about the promotion and I walked away knowing we had a solid plan of action in place to keep a dedicated employee continuing to grow in his career.

    However, one important thing to note is that just because we had a conscious and constructive conversation, it doesn't mean that there won't be consequences. For example, we had a plan in place for this employee to study, discuss, and implement leadership growth. Whether he chose to do that or not was not something I was going to become attached to. He may choose to grow in his leadership and be eligible for a promotion in a year. Or, he may choose not to, and will stay in his role or perhaps exit the organization. Do not confuse consciousness with complacency. We must still lead and act in the 100% external world.

7. REFLECT ON LESSONS FOR NEXT TIME

One final step for any conscious communication is reflection on the conversation, meeting, or email exchange. If you want to continue to grow spiritually, taking a look at what went well and what could be improved upon is helpful. Perhaps an activity you suggest could be taken company-wide. Maybe an employee shared valuable feedback with you that will change your communication in the future. Whatever it is, there is likely at least one thing that you can improve in the future. That is how you will continue to grow as a leader.

20

Conscious Leadership

The next generation of leaders is just as committed to their spiritual growth as they are to branding, business plans, and the bottom line.
　　　　　　　　　　　　　—Adam Hergenrother
　　　　　　　(Yes, I did just quote myself again.)

By the very fact that you are reading this book, you can see that building conscious or holistic businesses are gaining momentum. People want to partner with companies that take the whole person into account. They want to go to work somewhere they can truly be themselves and be celebrated for it. They want to work smart and have their hard work matter. This new era of companies will require conscious leaders. But what does being a conscious leader even mean?

Conscious leadership is made up of three main areas: awareness, knowing that you can engage with the mind as a tool but don't have to be ruled by it, and being able to stay centered no matter what comes your way.

There are eight signs that you are a conscious leader or that you are working with one. You can also start to develop your conscious leadership skills by reviewing the signs listed below.

1. CONSCIOUS LEADERS STAY NEUTRAL.

   Building a business and leading a team can certainly be a test of your patience, willpower, resilience, resolve, emotional fitness, and more. Which means it's the perfect place to practice staying neutral! When you have clients calling to complain about an employee—you stay neutral and centered. When your team just hit their biggest month of sales yet—you stay neutral and centered. This just means that you are dealing with your team and business without allowing your energy to get disturbed (positively or negatively).

   Warning: Do not mistake staying neutral with being indifferent. Rather, staying neutral simply allows you to listen, respond, make decisions, and act with increased clarity and better judgment.

2. CONSCIOUS LEADERS ARE VERY SELF-AWARE.

   To be a conscious leader means being a self-aware leader. Self-awareness comes from a commitment to questioning who you are and your motivations. It means studying your behavior and personality, and it means being willing to go inward and look at your flaws and strengths without judgment.

   These leaders know who they are, how and why they act the way they do, where they tend to push boundaries, when they look for loopholes, how they communicate, and much more. By being self-aware, these leaders play to their strengths instead of working on improving their weaknesses. And they teach and encourage their team members to do the same.

3. CONSCIOUS LEADERS SERVE AND CONTRIBUTE.

Conscious leaders are not concerned with what they can "get" from their team and their business, but rather about how they can serve and contribute. As Zig Zigler said, "You can have everything in life you want, if you will just help other people get what they want." Conscious leaders know this and make it a part of their day—every day.

If you need a quick practice to ensure you keep serving and contributing at the top of your mind, try this: Every time you pick up the phone, open a door, or get out of your car, use it as a sign-post to remind you that you are here on earth, at the office, on that phone call, in order to serve whomever is in front of you. From that foundation of servant leadership, a conscious business with other conscious leaders can be born.

4. CONSCIOUS LEADERS LET GO OF THE OUTCOME.

As a leader, it's really important to know what you can and can't control. You can control how tactical and comprehensive your career development programs are. You can't control whether or not your employees take advantage of them. Conscious leaders let go of the outcome of who does what, how people respond, or even how a decision turns out. Instead, they focus on their actions and activities in the moment. In addition, conscious leaders let go of the personal need to be right or for a particular outcome to come to fruition. In the example above, a leader may let go of the outcome of their employees putting in for a promotion. However, that leader will still make sure they are providing the coaching, training, and accountability to set their employees up for as much success as possible. They will create a clear path. Invest in continuing education. Give encouragement and tough love when needed. What they won't do is fill out the applications or write their employees' resumes for them, nor will they get personally attached to whether or not they do take action. When conscious leaders let go of the outcome, it allows them to remain clear, calm, and neutral for whatever else might come their way.

5. CONSCIOUS LEADERS DO NOT BOTHER THEMSELVES ABOUT THE MOMENT.
   Much like letting go of the outcome, conscious leaders understand that whatever moment, challenge, or experience is in front of them is not the problem. What *is* the problem is that you are bothering or disturbing yourself over the moment in front of you.

   Your Vice President is late for another meeting? A client leaves an unfavorable review? Your assistant double-books you again? Sure, those are all less-than-ideal situations. But think about this. A Vice President working at another company who is late to their meeting doesn't bother you—it's not even on your radar! Which means the situation with your VP in and of itself isn't the issue. What is at issue is your reaction, response, and mental gymnastics about the issue. You end up bothering yourself!

But conscious leaders do not bother themselves about the moment. They stay neutral. They let go of the outcome. They get clear on how to separate their personal self from the issue at hand. And then they get to work serving the moment (and the rest of their team) to the best of their ability. Yes, this may mean speaking to an employee about their performance or even firing someone, but it is all done consciously and from a centered place.

6. CONSCIOUS LEADERS ARE CURIOUS.
   One of the cornerstone habits of a conscious leader is staying open-minded and open-hearted. Cultivating curiosity is key. Great leaders listen and ask questions in order to find common ground on any topic. By being open to listening to (and encouraging) different perspectives, ideas, and viewpoints, leaders will ultimately make better decisions for their organizations.

7. CONSCIOUS LEADERS HAVE A CLEAR VISION.
   Having a clear vision is one of the three most important things a leader must do. This is a good time to go back to Chapter 18 and revisit your MVVBP. What are your guiding principles? What do you value? How does your company live out this vision? It is your job to spread the vision through every conversation, in every interaction with the media, and through social media, marketing and branding. Some people will love it (and you), and some

people will hate it. But by sharing the vision, you will attract the people who should be in your life and who will help you grow your business.

The more inner work you do, the stronger and more clear your vision will become because it will be aligned with your true self. Do the work to get this clarity. Your business will thank you for it.

8. CONSCIOUS LEADERS LEAD THEMSELVES FIRST. Guess what? Trying to force people to do what you want or need them to do is not leadership, and it will not get you very far in business or in life. Leading yourself at the highest level so people want to be around you and follow your example is what makes an outstanding leader and great business. Leadership is influence. And one of the best ways to influence others is to lead yourself first. Self-leadership precedes leadership.

I, like many others, became an entrepreneur because I wanted freedom. However, I quickly learned that, without daily routines, habits and structure, my business would end up owning me and my time instead of the other way around.

Make it a priority to invest in your personal and professional growth. Study leadership principles, read books, listen to podcasts, meditate, journal, fuel your body with proper nutrition, take a cold plunge, sleep well, and exercise—every day. Setting your intentions, your vision, and following through with your plan doesn't just help you grow, it helps everyone around you level up too.

A leader who knows how to lead themselves to bigger

and better things in life and business pushes themselves to do what they do part in service to those who depend on them. People watch leaders more than they ever listen to what they say. So, I'll ask you, how are you showing up?

When you talk about your early morning hike, run, or yoga class, or mention AHAs from a podcast, course you are taking, or book you are reading—others will sit up and take note. You've probably done this same thing! Have you ever heard someone you look up to talk about yoga (or something of the sort) and suddenly you are searching Google for a local hot yoga studio? That's self-leadership in action. When you better yourself, you better those around you. And there is no better way to lead yourself first than by focusing on your internal world and sharing those experiences with others.

Conscious leaders who truly embody and practice the above best practices are the leaders who will thrive and grow in any economic market. They are the leaders who will be able to effect change and lead their businesses and entire industries. When you show up as the best and most conscious version of yourself, you influence others to do the same and create an inclusive space for growth and expansion.

Part Four
Absolute Freedom

Letting Go

It is said that before entering the sea
a river trembles with fear.
She looks back at the path she has traveled,
from the peaks of the mountains,
the long winding road crossing forests and villages.
And in front of her,
she sees an ocean so vast,
that to enter
there seems nothing more than to disappear forever.
But there is no way back.
Nobody can go back.
To go back is impossible in existence.
The river needs to take the risk
of entering the ocean
because only then will fear disappear,
because that's where the river will know
it's not about disappearing into the ocean,
but of becoming the ocean.

—Khalil Gibran, "Fear"

Whether it's at home or in a professional work environment, creating a place where people can explore their inner selves is a powerful thing. It allows them to speak their truth, share their worries and challenges, celebrate their successes, and do it all from a place of non-judgment of self and others. Which leads us to one of the most challenging parts of personal and spiritual growth: letting go.

When I was in my twenties, I was still trying to run away from the overweight underachiever I had been for much of my teens. I did whatever was necessary to not be seen as that person, so I created a new identity: the guy who threw the best college parties. A gym-aholic who also trained in MMA and won two fights. A three-piece suit wearing businessman. The REALTOR with a bright orange wrapped Hummer with my face and name plastered across the side. A person who went after all of the individual awards and accolades to prove to myself and the world that I had made it, that I was successful, that I was enough.

I was running away from who I was that I didn't like, and I tried on many different identities along the way. There is nothing wrong with modeling your behavior or habits after people whom you admire, but eventually you need to find your own way. And the only way to really do this is to let go of who you think you are, or who you think you are supposed to be. To stop running away from who you were and to start running toward who you really are and who you want to become.

So, what stops people from truly letting go and living their most true and authentic life? Fear.

WHAT STOPS PEOPLE FROM LETTING GO?

What's interesting about the emotion of fear is that it can manifest itself in so many different ways. There are several dictionary definitions of fear: "a distressing emotion aroused by impending danger, evil, pain, etc., whether the threat is real or imagined;" "to have a reverential awe of;" "to be afraid and worried;" and "an unpleasant emotion caused by the belief that someone or something is dangerous."

Let's break it down even further. There is primal fear, the distressing emotion you feel when there is real and imminent danger (e.g. you're being chased by a tiger). Then there is psychological fear, the worry or unpleasant emotion that arises because you believe something is dangerous or will cause pain (e.g. speaking in front of a thousand of your peers).

In today's world, we don't experience primal fear very often. And even if we do, there is no "activated mind" in this state. You immediately go into a state of flow: fight, flight, freeze, or fawn. For example, if your house were burning, your primal fear would kick in and you would either: 1) run out of the house, 2) grab a fire extinguisher and try to put out the fire, or 3) become paralyzed and wait for someone to tell you to run or come rescue you. Fawning (immediately trying to please to avoid conflict or any further danger) doesn't really come into play in this scenario. However, it can be helpful when faced with other sorts of threatening situations, such as a robbery or an intoxicated person. The point here is that your mind shuts "off" and your body and instincts go into action. You're not going to your mind to start narrating a story, telling you about your preferences, and what you want to happen. It's all flow state.

Now, psychological fear is what we most often experience in this day and age. Psychological fear is all based on our needs, preferences, and our idea of how the world should be. This is where we can experience some real growth! Psychological fear comes down to two concepts:

1. I get worried, anxious, stressed, and scared that I won't get what I want.
2. I get worried, anxious, stressed, and scared that I will get what I don't want.

Let's say you're on a family vacation on the other side of the country, yet all you can think about is how worried you would be if your house burned down. Did you remember to turn off the oven? Did you leave anything plugged in that might overheat? Were there thunderstorms in the forecast? What if lightning strikes the house? Will it be protected? Did we remember to renew our insurance policy? What kind of coverage do we have? Do we have any gas cans in the garage?

You may physically be kayaking down the Colorado River through the Grand Canyon, but you are really back at home in South Carolina because your fear brought you there. It's a self-generated problem that doesn't really exist!

When you are stuck in your fear (and in your mind), it feels so real and you become so convinced that this is perfectly normal. Why wouldn't you have fear, right? But you need to see it for what it is. You have a problem. And no, it's not the possibility of your house burning down while you're gone on vacation. The problem is that you are still looking for the outside to make you feel okay. You are afraid that you will get something that you don't want. And when you're thinking this, you are essentially saying that you won't be able to handle it or that you won't be okay if something in the external world doesn't go your way.

The minute you recognize that these psychological needs do not need to be met in order to have joy, be creative, or be at peace, then you are free to live fully in this world and watch the world do its dance. Until then, you will always suffer from not getting what you want or getting what you don't want.

In the end, the way out is to be aware of this. Watch your psychological fear unfold. Accept it. Surrender. Let go. You can watch a part of yourself get nervous or scared. But you are the one watching. Soon enough, the fear moves through you and you regain your seat of consciousness. You have accepted that life will do its dance and you are okay with everything. It's truly the way out.

If you are okay with everything, you are fearless.

The ultimate goal is to be okay with everything. If you're not there yet, start by being okay with the awareness that you're experiencing the feeling and then make the choice to let it go.

SAYING GOODBYE TO WHO YOU THOUGHT YOU WERE

I know I've said it before, but I will say it again: letting go and truly surrendering to life is the hardest thing you'll ever do. But you're here. You're doing the work. Don't stop now. You may feel like you are teetering on the edge of a cliff, because part of you *is* (your ego). You are upending your current beliefs of reality, questioning who you are and why you are here, and therefore a part of you is being removed. It causes a lot of turbulence in life, particularly if you have already spent decades creating a version of yourself that you want to show to the world. Letting go of that is not easy.

Let's hear from one of my coaching clients. I bet their feelings will sound very familiar:

> Like many of us, I've spent so much of my life building the exterior to look and seem exactly as I wanted to be perceived. Sometimes where I truly believed the image I'd created was what I wanted, and if others could accept me for all of these things I can do and achieve, then maybe I could accept myself too. The more I "perfected" the creation, the emptier and more unfulfilled I felt... often having to coach myself into believing that this outward portrayal would be the key to filling the inner hole.... and that's really when the conflict within myself began. It was a mindfuck...because there I was "being"

the creation that I thought I needed to fix the inside....
and all I could feel was confusion and disappointment
that I sold my soul to become what I thought would
complete me, and in reality I had hit a very fragmented
bottom... So then the biggest fear of them all—"I'd be
found out as a fraud"....and I couldn't possibly undo what
I'd done....because ultimately I'd have to face "the truth"
and it was too much for my ego to bear.... That's about
as brief as I can summarize the downward spiral, and
undoing of the past 3-4 years (maybe longer).

So fast forward to the journey—when I finally
surrendered and said I am not my ego, nor the image
I've created....I am me, and I need to find out who "me"
is again. The only way I could conceptually do this, was
to "wipe the slate clean," quit everything without the fear
of what people would think of me, and go into an early
partial retirement. (I still feel like a loser admitting I quit
my life because I couldn't function in the high stress/
anxious, mask wearing world I'd created! Ding: ego!)

So I'm writing to say that it's all very slowly finally
starting to happen and make sense. Letting go of who I
think the world wants me to be, and just being okay with
not knowing what's next, being okay with knowing that
tomorrow the most impressive thing I will accomplish will
be following my diet and exercise exactly as scheduled...
and maybe submitting my taxes to my CPA. I am not
my actions, my preferences, nor what I do or create. I
am finally learning discipline and consistency like I never
have before, and it feels good that I am building the life I
want to live...not the life I think people want me to live...
so that maybe they will like me. :). But most importantly,
I'm not fighting any of the feelings...I feel them, and

move along with my day. I finally let go of the rope...
and thought maybe I should try a different strategy 'cause
my hands have rope burn, y'all! ;) So dang scary! How
do I not know who I am and what I want...that's what
all of this boils down to. I thought I wanted that...and I
lost myself creating it...only frantically trying to find the
control/alt/delete function.

The beauty of what this individual shared is that this is a universal
human experience, that she has just done enough inner work to
recognize and explore. You may be wrestling with saying goodbye to
who you thought you were or who you were told you are supposed to
be. But all you have to do is let go of the rope.

Imagine you were playing tug of war against a professional football
team—yes, all fifty-three of them. You are giving it everything you've
got. Your feet are buried in the dirt. Your hands are burning and
bleeding. You are gritting your teeth. You are holding so tightly to the
rope, to wanting to win, to everything you thought you knew. You
know that as soon as you let go, you will no longer be in control and
you will have lost everything. You will never be free if you let go of
the rope.

And yet… as you are fighting for your life, holding on to the rope, a
spiritual teacher comes along and taps you on the shoulder and says,
"Just let go of the rope." You fight back and say that's impossible. If
you do, you'll lose! The spiritual teacher says again, "Just let go of the
rope." Finally, you let go of the rope. You take a deep breath. You
stand up straight. You are free.

Turns out, you were free all along. You just had to let go of your
identity, your mind, and your ego. When you let go of the rope, your
ego isn't controlling you anymore. You are you. And you are free.

22

Aim Higher

Aim high, aim at the highest, and all lower aims are thereby achieved. It is looking below on the stormy sea of differences that make you sink. Look up, beyond these and see the One Glorious Real, and you are saved.

—Ramana Maharshi

Letting go is the ultimate surrender. Letting go is a combination of the following: not being attached to outcomes, needing nothing, surrendering preferences and expectations, accepting the present, relinquishing the ego, and keeping an open heart—all things we've been talking about throughout this book.

There are a lot of things that keep us from letting go—not the least of which is fear. Once you have brought awareness to your fears and your ego, you can begin to practice letting go at any and all moments in your life.

This does not preclude you from setting goals in the external world, as long as you don't attach yourself to the outcome. We're working with a 200% life here! It is helpful to have a target in the external world, as long as you set your aim higher in the internal world. Letting go will help get you there.

WHAT DOES LETTING GO FEEL LIKE?

When you feel a disturbance and a shift of energy come into your mind and body, one of three things will usually happen: suppression, expression, or truly letting go and surrendering. Let's take a look at each of these.

1. SUPPRESSION

When your energy and emotions are taking you over, one choice is to suppress the energy. This is a terrible idea, and yet sometimes it's necessary. I rarely, if ever, want to suppress any event because that means I will have to deal with it later on as a stored energy pattern because I pushed it down. It's like you've taken the energy and pushed it back inside you with both hands and unconsciously said, "Nope. Not going to express this or deal with this energy right now. I'll just set that aside for later." So, you store the energy but it inevitably shows back up, usually when you least expect or want it to.

However, there are times when you do need to table the energy or emotion for later. Do not suppress it, just delay its release intentionally until you can get to a time and place where you can work through it, sit with it, and release it. For example, if your boss gives you really harsh feedback, you may get defensive and want to yell and curse the day she was born. Instead, you can choose to suppress it in the moment, take a walk around the block or go back to your office to deal with the energy release. Delay, but don't suppress it.

2. EXPRESSION

When you feel negative energy and emotions arise, you can tell the other party how you feel and, most likely, you'll feel better. Why? Because you've released the energy (maybe through a conversion, text message, or yelling). The energy needed to go somewhere, so you expressed it. People express energy in all sorts of ways, both constructive and unconstructive, such as exercise, punching a pillow, drinking alcohol, yelling, or eating.

By expressing the energy, you did release the vibrational code, but you didn't deal with the root cause of the issue. Oftentimes, depending on your means of release, you can make the situation worse by involving someone else in the negative expression of your energy. In fact, I've heard that spiritual masters used to teach their students that while they were still in control, but were starting to feel the urge to express their emotions, and they knew that they were about to be taken over by them, that their best course of action was to simply run away. Run away! These spiritual masters actually believed it was better to run away than to express the energy in the moment, when you are no longer in control.

3. SURRENDER

Finally, you can choose to surrender to the energy and emotion and allow it to pass. If you sit with it and allow the energy to move through you (without going to your mind to make you feel better), then it will be gone forever.

Don't focus on the emotion itself. It's a mistake to try to make your anger or sadness relax. It will usually make it worse, because you're putting your attention on the energy that you are trying to release. Instead, separate yourself from the emotion and feel the energy in front of you. Just like when you were holding on to the rope, let it slip through your fingers. Keep letting go. Let go of trying to hold the energy in place and "fix" it. Just let it go.

What people want to do is push against the feeling in order to make it go away. It's like there are 50 MPH winds at the top of a mountain, whipping your hair and pushing you backwards. So you grab a 4-foot by 8-foot piece of plywood and hold it in front of you to protect yourself from the wind. You're struggling to keep the plywood in place, it keeps twisting and turning, and it's taking all your strength to hold it up against the wind. How much more energy does this take? When all you really have to do is accept that the wind is blowing your hair and wait for the wind to die down.

Even when you begin to relax behind the emotion, the feeling may intensify. It can get really uncomfortable inside, to the point where every part of you wants to push the event back down (see suppression) or blurt out a "Screw you!" to your business partner (see expression). But you don't. You allow the event to keep traveling further down inside you, towards the real you, a place where you've never felt events at this depth before. It feels burning hot, as if it's piercing a part of you. But you continue to sit with it. You continue to relax behind the energy. The energy gets closer and closer and hotter and hotter, and then, magically, it's gone. That is when you know the event and energy has moved through you. Relief washes over you. A part of you has died. A part of you is gone forever and in its place a truer, more conscious you is born.

As you start to let go of the smaller things (like the fact that your friend never texts you back or the president of your company always gives you bottles of wine for celebrations even though you've been sober for six years), bigger events will arise. They will intensify in heat and discomfort. When this happens to me, I feel a big welling up inside and I sit with it. I can physically feel the energy event making its way from my lower abdomen to my stomach and then up through my heart, my throat, and then exiting through my mouth or between my eyes. It's very real, yet I don't see anything. Most of the time, these large energy releases cause me to gag and they take my breath away for a few seconds, up to twenty seconds at a time. The interesting thing is that any moment, I can stop it. I can suppress it. I can pause the energy release and push it back down. But I know that anytime I have a chance to get rid of this type of energy, a part of me, I do it, whatever the cost. It is the pain that removes all pain.

Don't let this scare you. It's a good thing! The key is to continue to sit behind the energy and let shakti (source energy) do her dance. Don't try to engage with the energy. Thank it for showing up and thank it for leaving.

Remember, some of these events that are more intense and painful could have been something that happened to you when you were eight and you didn't get picked for the football game. It causes you a ton of pain and because you never processed it, it was stored as a samskara. And then it randomly comes back up when you get cut off by another car. Or it could be a series of events that happened throughout your life, like snowflakes, and got stored as one giant snowball. It's impossible to determine which snowflake caused the emotions to come up. That is why sometimes when we feel massive anger, we don't always know what causes it. There could be a million smaller events that led to the one event that made you angry. This is why we can't go to the mind to ask it to help us figure out what is going on. It can't help in these situations. And does it really matter where it came from? I think not. If you relax behind the energy and truly let it go, it will never bother you again.

YOUR AIM

It's also very important that you don't add any new events as you are releasing the old ones. This is why it's critical to feel the event in the moment, to feel the discomfort of it, to let it move through you, and to get clear. When we allow the event to move all the way through us in real time, we don't have to worry about adding even more emotion and energy to the event, having it be stored as a samskara, or letting it go at a later date.

Each day, you should set your aim on two things. One, getting rid of stored energy patterns, and two, making sure you don't add any more in.

For example, recently, one of my leaders came into my office to discuss a deal we were negotiating. I didn't like the terms he was outlining and I got triggered. In that moment, I "lost it." I threw in the proverbial towel and told him to take the deal, that I was getting screwed, and the whole situation sucked anyway, or something to that effect. The egoic side of me took over and "I" was no longer present to communicate effectively, to say the least. As soon as it happened, I knew it. I knew I had allowed my ego to take over.

Immediately, I started working on how fast I could get back to center, and then handle the deal and my employee. I let go. I got behind the energy. I let go some more. I closed my eyes and allowed the event to move through me. It wanted to stay there. It sucked. It hurt. My mind was going crazy, but I just kept relaxing. About five minutes later, the energy had moved through. I picked up my phone, apologized to my colleague, dealt with the contract, and moved on.

The whole event was only fifteen minutes. Now, to be clear, I still had to sit with this event and it still took everything I had to call and apologize and to see the issue with clarity. Every part of my ego wanted me to fight, punch, yell, say why I was right, etc. And before my spiritual journey, I would have done all of that. This might have been something I held on to for months, and during that time I would have made it worse by allowing my ego to take over.

Aim higher means relaxing and releasing at all times. When you slip, and you all will, ask yourself how quickly you can get back and release the event.

Give it a try. The next time you are fighting with your partner, see how difficult it would be for "You" to give them a hug. Could you do it? I mean, you love them, right? Why can't you hug them? You just hugged them an hour ago and told them how much you love and appreciate them. But at this moment? Hell, no! What's changed? Your ego and energy have gone lower and taken over.

Can you relax behind the energy enough that you are able to hug them? That is spiritual strength. That is personal growth.

You'll feel a pull for the ego to take over. In fact, you'll feel it constantly. It's a feeling that there is a lower part of you trying to pull you down into a lesser version of yourself. Most of the time it succeeds. There is a tug, a pull. When you feel that, that's when you relax. You relax to the energy that is trying to pull you from your seat of centeredness, your seat of consciousness.

When you let go, when you surrender, you are surrendering to the pull, to the tendency to go lower and act from that place. As you surrender, you become aware that there is another pull, a pull that you've never felt before. It's way higher than anything else you've ever experienced. Get lost in that pull, it's pulling you upward and keeping your aim higher. That is liberation.

CONCLUSION

Absolute Freedom

There are only two mistakes one can make along the road to truth; not going all the way, and not starting.

—Buddha

I've always been driven by freedom. Most entrepreneurs, business owners, and leaders I know are too. In my first book (*The Founder & The Force Multiplier: How Entrepreneurs and Executive Assistants Achieve More Together*, written in 2019), I actually wrote, "Freedom is what drives every decision I make. Freedom is what gets me up at 4:30 a.m. and keeps me inspired all day. Financial freedom. Freedom to give by richly blessing other people's lives. Physical freedom. Spiritual freedom to truly understand and accept myself and others. Social freedom to experience the journey of life with other people when and where I choose. It's all about freedom."

But, I only really hit on half of it there. Well, 100% of it, that is. I was mostly referring to the external world. Where we believe that money is freedom, time is freedom, that knowledge is freedom, that a certain position at our company is freedom, that travel is freedom, that our words are freedom, or that doing whatever we want to do whenever we want to do it is freedom.

Sure, there is some relative truth to all of the above. But it's not the whole truth about freedom. It's not the absolute truth. It's not absolute freedom.

I have discovered the difference between relative and absolute freedom on my spiritual journey and I hope you have, too, by reading this book.

Absolute freedom is found in the other 100% of life—your inner world.

Absolute freedom is an internal state of being and is not affected by money or knowledge or anything in the external world. It comes purely from a state within your consciousness that is clear and devoid of any negative energy. Absolute freedom is being able to walk around the world watching your ego instead of being pulled in every direction by it or responding to your mind. It's living from a place of surrender, absolute well-being and peace, despite having a disturbed ego. That's the absolute freedom people are looking for.

Absolute freedom is the ability to walk around the world without ever being disturbed by anything. Absolute freedom is a state of being that can not be achieved through thoughts or words, only through direct experience. Absolute freedom is a knowing. And the truth of life lies within that knowing. It is the essence of who you really are.

FREEDOM FROM YOURSELF

Life is the ultimate teacher. Every moment, there is an opportunity to practice letting go. Let go of the part of you that is keeping you from accepting or enjoying the experience.

When you let go, the world starts unfolding for you. When you become untethered from your desires and expectations, the world rises up to meet you where you are at and support you along the way. Your life becomes more natural, more aligned, more spontaneous, and more effortless.

Do you know how you catch a wild monkey? No, it's not some trick question or joke just waiting for a punchline. It's actually pretty interesting.

Take a wooden box or large container and drill a hole into the side of it—just large enough for a monkey to put its hand through. Place a few bananas or other fruit inside the container. Wait. Eventually, a monkey will come along and put its hand through the hole and grab ahold of the banana. Because the banana is much too large to fit through the hole, the monkey will stay there, grasping the banana, just stuck. You walk up to the monkey. Monkey caught.

Yes, yes, there is a lesson in this story. The monkey was free all along. All it had to do was let go of the banana. Dropping the banana means the monkey would have been free and not caught. But the monkey was so worried about losing the banana that it was willing to risk its freedom.

And that's exactly what we do, isn't it?

We say we want absolute freedom, peace, and joy in our lives, yet we are still holding so tightly to our external worlds, to our identity, our relationships, our career, our money, etc. We are afraid that if we let go, our entire world will fall apart. And it might—at least the world as we knew it. But by letting go, a whole new world of experiences and existence awaits. You just have to let go of the banana.

In some of the early stages of spiritual growth, we can get stuck in the intellect. While well-intentioned, analyzing your thoughts and feelings can keep you stuck in old patterns of behaviors or stuck in the past in general. We want to figure out why we think the way we do, what causes our emotions, and we dive deeper and deeper to find out the root cause of our "problems." This can be helpful, to a point. The reality is, you don't really need to understand all of it. Your mind doesn't need to be fully understood. Instead of analyzing it all, what if you just let it go? You acknowledge that you have a problem, let it move through you, release it, and then handle the next moment in front of you.

Life is our teacher and if we accept that we are the student, I promise, life will give us exactly the homework we need.

In the Pixar movie *Soul*, jazz pianist Joe Gardner believes that death has denied him from achieving his purpose in life, and he is determined to get back to earth to fulfill his destiny. There is a really beautiful moment at the end of the movie when Counselor Jerry A from The Great Beyond asks Joe what he is going to do now that he has helped 22 find their purpose and he has returned to his body after being in a coma. Counselor Jerry A asks, "How are you going to spend your life?" And Joe replies, "I'm not sure. But I do know I'm going to live every minute of it."

That is true surrender. It's relatively inconsequential what your purpose or passions or likes or dislikes are in the grand scheme of things. It's about letting all of that go and just living!

Liberation is a process that happens to you, not by you.

As you continue on your spiritual growth journey, remember that. Stop trying to make "it" happen. As long as you are trying to become, trying to get something (even if that is enlightenment!), trying to attain something, you are quite literally moving away from the Truth itself. That if you have to think about it, it's not truly letting go. By releasing and relaxing, transformation comes to you. Energy will shift within you, not because you told it to, but because you allowed it to happen by just being. Let go of expectations. Don't try to let go, just let it be.

You are not getting freedom *for* yourself, you are getting freedom *from* yourself.

This state of freedom happens when, even for a moment, and for no reason, you are freed from within by this incredible spirit/divine energy that consumes your entire body. The energy is so strong that there is nothing in the external world that could take your attention away from the energy flowing inside of you. This is when you know that the world has lost its salt, that the world has lost its taste so that you no longer need to categorize things as likes and dislikes or arrange the world in a way that will personally serve your needs.

Yes, you will still work, build businesses, interact with family and friends, have wonderful relationships, and lean into life, but you are not manipulating the outside world to serve you. You aren't even serving others. You are just acting with the flow of life. Your energy within is so effortless and powerful that you are free.

Take a deep breath and allow that energy to move through you.

Your 200% life awaits.

Keep Going!

THE 200% LIFE NEWSLETTER

Don't let your learning and growth stop when you finish this book! Join me each week as I share tools and resources to help you accelerate both your inner and outer growth. From the latest research on effective leadership strategies to philosophical insights on what it means to live a more fulfilling life, I share anything that might help you maximize your 200% life.

Subscribe to the newsletter at:
adamhergenrother.com/newsletter

THE 200% LIFE PODCAST

The material success we experience in our outer worlds is only 100% of the puzzle. We also need to tap into the 100% of life that is our inner world (meditation, the ego, identities and self-concepts, etc.) to truly experience the life of fulfillment, joy, and enthusiasm we all strive for. We call this the 200% life.

The 200% Life podcast is for the leaders and high achievers who have reached success on the outside and still feel like something is missing in their life. We dig deep into the tough questions about life and business and leadership. You're going to learn how to get and give anything you want in life by mastering your inner world first. After all, business is nothing but a conduit for your personal growth. Need nothing. Enjoy everything!

Listen to the podcast here:
adamhergenrother.com/podcast

LEARN MORE ABOUT MICHAEL SINGER

To keep deepening your inner work, I would highly recommend reading all of Michael Singer's books; including, *The Untethered Soul, The Surrender Experiment,* and *Living Untethered.* If you're new to his work, *The Surrender Experiment* is a great place to start. If you're ready to do very deep inner work, be sure to listen to the free talks he shares three times a week on the Temple of the Universe website: https://tou.org/talks/

A REQUEST

If you like this book and found it helpful, could you please take a moment to leave a review on Amazon? Every review makes a difference and will help this book and the 200% life philosophy reach more people. Just imagine what the world would look like once more people started experiencing the 200% life! Thank you in advance for your review. I read each one and I am excited and humbled every time I see one come through.

LET'S CONNECT!

Email: hello@adamhergenrother.com
Instagram: @adamhergenrother
LinkedIn: Adam Hergenrother
Facebook: Adam Hergenrother

Sources Cited

Below are the sources cited throughout the book
in order of appearance.

The Power of Now: A Guide to Spiritual Enlightenment, Eckhart Tolle,
New World Library, 2004.

The Science of Being and Art of Living: Transcendental Meditation,
Maharishi Mahesh Yogi, Signet, 1968.

"The Watcher," Season 1, Episode 1, "Welcome, Friends,"
10/13/2022.

The Evolving Self: Problem and Process in Human Development,
Robert Kegan, Harvard UP, 1982.

"The Road Not Taken," *Mountain Interval,* Robert Frost, Henry
Holt, 1916.

*Toward a Psychology of Awakening: Buddhism, Psychotherapy, and
the Path of Personal and Spiritual Transformation,* John Welwood,
Shambhala, 2002.

The Bhagavad Gita, 2nd Edition, Introduced and Translated by
Eknath Easwaran, Nilgiri Press, 2007.

The Untethered Soul: The Journey Beyond Yourself, Michael A. Singer, New Harbinger Publications, 2007.

The Most Important Thing, Volume 1, Discovering Truth at the Heart of Life, Adyashanti, Sounds True, 2019.

"Power is influence…" James Clear, X post, 02/10/2020.

Yogapedia, "Samskara," July 31, 2020, www.yogapedia.com/ definition/5748/samskara.

Untamed, Glennon Doyle, The Dial Press, 2020.

Thy Mind, O Human, "The Evolution of Ego in the Allegory of Adam & Eve," Bryce Haymond, www.thymindoman.com/the-evolution-of-ego-in-the-allegory-of-adam-eve/.

Hsin-Hsin Mind: Verses on the Faith-Mind, Seng T'San, White Pine Press, 2001.

The Culture of Counter-Culture: Edited Transcripts, Alan Wilson Watts, C. E. Tuttle Co., 1998.

Eleven Rings: The Soul of Success, Phil Jackson, Penguin Press, 2013.

Notes on a Nervous Planet, Matt Haig, Penguin Press, 2019.

The Tibetan Book of Living and Dying, Sogyal Rinpoche, HarperSanFrancisco, 1992.

"Take care of your body…" Jim Rohn, Facebook post, 07/30/2016.

Love in the Time of Cholera, Gabriel García Márquez, Vintage, 2007.

Principles: Life and Work, Ray Dalio, Avid Reader Press / Simon & Schuster, 2017.

Fearless Soul, "21 Insightful Vishen Lakhiani Quotes on the Power of the Mind," TEAMSOUL, https://iamfearlesssoul.com/vishen-lakhiani-quotes/.

"Fear," Kahlil Gibran, poem in public domain.

"Soul," Pixar, 2020.

About the Authors

ADAM HERGENROTHER is an entrepreneur at heart. He is the Founder & CEO of the thriving organization, Adam Hergenrother Companies, which includes several organizations ranging from a national real estate company to real estate development, to leadership coaching and training. He is passionate about using business to transform lives and believes that when you focus on leading yourself first, the business results will follow. When he's not leading and growing his organizations or working on his inner growth, you can find Adam in the Vermont mountains with his wife, Sarah, and three children, Sienna, Asher, and Madelyn.

HALLIE WARNER joined forces with Adam in late 2010, first as his Executive Assistant, then serving alongside Adam as his Chief of Staff for almost a decade. This is the second book that Hallie has written with Adam. When she is not coaching, consulting, or writing, Hallie is probably reading or making a list. Hallie lives in Vermont with her husband, Bill, and their dogs, Enzo and Stella.

One Last Thing Before You Go!

If you found value in this book, please take *one minute* to leave a review on the platform where you purchased it.

The very best compliment an author can receive is a positive book review. We always look forward to reading what aha's and insights you gained from the book and are endlessly grateful for your support. We read every review!

Plus, by taking the time to reflect on what you just read, you increase your chances of long-term retention and can potentially impact another reader's life in a small but meaningful way.

Thank you for taking one minute to leave a review.

We appreciate your support in getting The 200% Life approach to business out into the world!